# GREEN BERETS IN THE VANGUARD

# GREEN BERETS IN THE VANGUARD

## Inside Special Forces, 1953–1963

### Chalmers Archer Jr.

Naval Institute Press

Annapolis, Maryland

Naval Institute Press
291 Wood Road
Annapolis, MD 21402

Library of Congress Cataloging-in-Publication Data
Archer, Chalmers, 1928-
    Green Berets in the vanguard : inside Special Forces, 1953-1963 /
Chalmers Archer, Jr.
        p. cm. — (Naval Institute special warfare series)
    ISBN 1-55750-023-1 (alk. paper)
    1. Archer, Chalmers, 1928- 2. United States. Army. Special
Forces—Biography. 3. Afro-American soldiers—Biography. I. Title. II.
Series.
    U53.A73 A3 2001
    356'.167'0973—dc21                                      00-051131

Printed in the United States of America on acid-free paper ∞
08 07 06 05 04 03 02 01  9 8 7 6 5 4 3 2
First printing

In memory of my mother, Eva Alcola Ratherford Archer, pioneer educator, librarian, and math teacher; my father, Mr. Chalmers Archer Sr., World War I artillery corporal and innovative farmer, noted for his untiring efforts in civil rights; and my sister Hermione Y. Anglin, a brilliant student while at Howard University and a federal Commerce Department administrator. They made lives better for all who knew them.

# Contents

# Preface

In 1952, when I was a twenty-three-year-old medical corpsman, I was assigned to the 10th Special Forces Group, U.S. Army, and sent to Fort Bragg, North Carolina, for six months of training at the Psychological Warfare Center (PWC). I had already been overseas for several years, in the Philippines and Okinawa. I considered myself to be the top trained medic in the U.S. Army and thought I might eventually become a sergeant major of a large hospital detachment. I had no idea how far I had to go or where, in fact, my career would take me.

Over the next fourteen years both I and the Special Forces evolved to maturity. My career goals took a sharp turn. I would always have a medical specialty, but as a member of the first group of soldiers to wear the Green Beret, a unique symbol of America's military pride.

Very few people got a close look at the activities of Special Forces in those early days; almost everything was a mystery. Except for the people directly involved in our training at the PWC and its special schools, such as the medical school at Fort Sam Houston, Texas, no one knew what we did. Thus, with this book, I can enable readers to look through a personal peephole for a view of a unique military culture in its formative stages.

This book records my firsthand view of Special Forces: what it was, what it did and how, and what it became in the years of my experience in it. From the beginning, we were intended to perform more as political scientists and trainers than as soldiers. Our credentials equaled the accreditation of U.S. military attachés. We were trained for and deployed in secret assignments, surreptitious military missions, and various forms of special warfare. We in turn trained indigenous peoples all over the world; many of us were multilingual. As trainers and then as warriors, we forged strong bonds with other nations. Our operations strongly influenced American international policy.

Special Forces was a high-risk enterprise, not only in the sense of mortality but in terms of military careers as well. It started as a vision—chiefly the vision of Lt. Col. Albert Scott Madding, whose special assistant I was privileged to be when he was the first commander of the 1st Special Forces Group. It started as a closely held secret, no place for publicity hounds. It evolved as a unit recognized for its extraordinary character: the 14th Special Forces Operational Detachment.

### How a Book Began

Safely locked in an old tin trunk at my mother's house, long before this book began, were 163 pages of manuscript, some of it in handwriting, some of it typed, written in my young adulthood. They represented a "closed book" in my life: my years of military service. Not coincidentally, they also represented a common custom in black families, of recording and telling of past experiences, lest they be lost to time. I am grateful for that, because when I began to write a memoir about the Special Forces, I had a firm foundation with which to start. My notes went all the way back to my USAF service in the Philippines and Okinawa.

Equally fortunate—and probably also a result of my family background—I have a storyteller's memory; I can recall all-day conversations in their essence and repeat them in detail. As a trainee at Fort Bragg and elsewhere, I found this gift invaluable, since note-taking was often forbidden in the classroom; we had to internalize lectures and training proceedings and write them up later. My technique was to make a complete story out of the main points.

The hours spent considering this project were times of intense reflection for me. My mind raced among three worlds: my current life, my military experiences in Vietnam, Laos, and other countries, and—because it has never left me—my childhood.

As I describe in my first book, *Growing Up Black in Rural Mississippi* (New York: Walker, 1992), it was a childhood both glorious and grim, delightfully free as country childhoods can be but shadowed by dangers in the surrounding white community. My parents' wisdom armed me for a career that would challenge, stimulate, and toughen me in ways they never dreamed of. In the field, in all kinds of threatening situations, I could hear their reassuring voices, point for point.

In thinking about my military career, I had to recall gunfire and death—reruns that I had harbored for over forty years. Although I never have flashbacks, in this process I was internally in turmoil; it was hard to keep my voice steady when I spoke to anyone about writing this book. We were highly trained fighting men whose engagements had profound effects on world politics. We fought; some of us died. And our primary mission, which was to train friendly troops in effective tactics, was clandestine, so it has never been widely understood or appreciated at home. Readers will remember that the period this memoir covers begins in 1952, under the Eisenhower administration. It was a different world.

At the time I was invited to recall those years in print, I was a full-time professor at North Virginia Community College in Alexandria—teaching friendly "troops" of young Virginians. My mind floated numbly around the book I was about to write. What would it mean? Why did I agree to do this?

Was it because everyone—especially the nation's youth—needs to know about the sacrifices that the Green Berets made and that they served not only with valor but also with compassion?

Was it because these men of the Green Berets performed missions that very few people knew about, under circumstances that earned them at least this tribute and much more?

Or was it my (deeply held) belief that any light shed on any phase of the Southeast Asian conflicts helps our nation recover from their effects?

Perhaps, simply, I wanted to review my experiences and lay some disturbing memories to rest. Perhaps, for some readers who share these memories, that will be reason enough.

# Acknowledgments

Many people helped with this book. While none of them is responsible to any extent at all for its shortcomings and errors, each helped to make it much better than it would otherwise be.

Only one, Sgt. Maj. Robert Bennett, U.S. Special Forces (Retired), was a member of my initial team. He helped in any way that he could, supplying documents and dates that I could never have obtained otherwise. As in our earlier days together, Sergeant Major Bennett remains a true Special Forces team player for whom I am eternally grateful.

I also relied on the recollections of Sgt. Maj. Harold Copeland, U.S. Special Forces (Ret.), a fellow unit member from 1954 to 1965, whose experiences closely mirrored mine.

First Sgt. Matthew L. Brown, U.S. Army (Ret.), served as my Research and Verification Officer during the entire book-writing project. An experienced Special Forces and combat noncommissioned officer, he assisted in countless ways.

Thanks to another special advisor, Horace Gerald Danner, Ph.D., Professor of English, University of Maryland University College, and Chief Master Sergeant, U.S. Air Force (Ret.).

To Col. Austin Frederick, U.S. Army (Ret.), goes special appreciation for his astute counsel and insight on the book's message.

Mrs. Dorothy P. Madding, wife of our commander, Lt. Col. Albert Scott Madding, supported our effort with enthusiasm, sharing family and other photos that offered special insight into 14th Special Forces activities through the years, as well as stories, recollections, and general information. I cannot do justice to her contribution.

Lt. Col. Wallace Johnson, U.S. Army Special Forces (Ret.), assisted in research to determine the direction of Special Forces objectives from the 1950s and later dates from his experience. Clyde J. Sincere Jr., U.S. Army Special Forces (Ret.), a Special Forces historian and author, contributed substantially to the book effort as well, by authenticating movements, dates, and other facts. My thanks to both.

I am also grateful for the contributions of my family, including my brother, Anselm J. F. Archer, my sister and brothers—Evelyn, Francis, and Vernon—and my nieces and nephews, Adrienne, Tamatha, Francis Jr., and Paul. And I am especially indebted to Sovanny Saray, for her undying support, loyalty, and faith.

Special thanks to archivist and publisher Stephen Sherman of the RADIX Press, for recommending that the Naval Institute Press consider publishing my Special Forces experiences. Mark Gatlin, then senior acquisitions editor at the Naval Institute Press, initiated the project, and Jeanne Pinault, my editor, brought it to completion; I thank them both. I am forever indebted to Ric Clark, publisher and owner of the Reconciliation Press, for his guidance and encouragement.

More thanks must go to the following coworkers and colleagues to whom I circulated the initial text: Kellie Blair, my student assistant at Northern Virginia Community College and Polytechnic Institute and State University; E. Nadine D. Boone, for her way of telling a story; Tom Banigan, long-time resident of Taiwan and frequent traveler throughout Asia; Maj. Bernard M. Hayes, for his photos; Emily H. Proctor, Charles A. Smith, and Della Rucker, for editorial support; Lt. Col. Edward A. Sawyer, U.S. Army (Ret.), for his comments on the future of the army; Col. Warren S. Smith, U.S. Army (Ret.), for his comprehensive grasp of Special Forces as it is today; and Barbara Laime-Williams, for her unfailing counsel, encouragement, and support.

# GREEN BERETS IN THE VANGUARD

# 1   *ASSIGNED TO SPECIAL FORCES, AIRBORNE*

I remember a feeling of excitement, awe, and anticipation on that bright morning in 1952. I was about to start my first six months at the Psychological Warfare Center, at Fort Bragg, home of the U.S. Army Special Forces. My home would be the eternally dingy military barracks in Smoke Bomb Hill, set in the beauty of North Carolina's fields, streams, and pines.

Special Forces was a new unit that had everybody at Fort Bragg raving. It was the one I had read and heard so much about. To tell the truth, though, I did not have a clue about what was going to happen next.

My current assignment was as a non-jumper or "leg" field first sergeant—sort of an assistant first sergeant, since there were no E-8s or E-9s at the time—with headquarters and Headquarters Company. My ultimate intention at this point was to become jump qualified and a full-fledged operational member of the Special Forces.

The men in my group—less than a dozen of us—stood at the beginning of an exceptional journey. Some of us would assume permanent Special Forces maintenance duties; others, administrative positions that supported Special Forces–type operations. Although uncertain about exactly what we would encounter, we all knew that Fort Bragg was something special.

None of us understood the magnitude of the effort for which we were preparing. We would be executing paramilitary operations in enemy-held and -controlled areas around the world. We were about to immerse ourselves in guerrilla warfare, escape and evasion, subversion, and sabotage, involving operations described as "low-visibility, surreptitious, or clandestine." We would be serving as the nucleus of the United States Special Forces and as the de facto trainers of the Special Forces of the Thai, Laotian, Korean, Chinese, Filipino, and Vietnamese armies.

As a result of our teaching, national counterinsurgency forces would learn how to penetrate and isolate enemy bases, disrupt lines of communication, attack hidden logistical support bases, gather intelligence, and perform numerous other operations. The Minox camera for gathering intelligence and the stiletto as a weapon would become essential parts of our standard operating gear. (It would be our headgear, though, that marked us as extraordinary soldiers.)

Moreover, none of us knew that we would be among the first units of a new kind of unconventional warrior. Nor did we realize that our performance in unconventional warfare would influence top-level decisions regarding foreign policy and other international matters.

I certainly did not have the faintest notion that my military future would become inextricably intertwined with the 77th Group, in which I would play a variety of roles, including trainer, medic, and cadre. Although my Air Force career had already taken me to Okinawa (twice) and the Philippines, with Special Forces I would travel farther—professionally, emotionally, and spiritually—than I could have imagined that day in 1952. I would even assist in designing the first Special Forces patch and help make that distinctive headgear our signature. None of us could have known that, before it was all over, my group would become part of the history of Southeast Asia. I was good at what I did and ready for anything, or I wouldn't have been there, but my crystal ball was no better than anybody else's.

Amazingly, we eventually came to redefine the concepts of warfare in our times. We would become the legendary Green Berets.

### The First Special Forces Commander

Col. Aaron S. Bank, a former Jedburgh commander, came from Korea to start the 10th Special Forces at Fort Bragg. Both he and Col. Russell Volckmann, another former OSS operative, envisioned Special Operations as a force multiplier, a bold idea that went counter to conventional concepts. They worked tirelessly to convince the army chiefs, who were unreceptive to unconventional warfare, as to its worth. They insisted that they could provide ideal forces for unconventional harassment and guerrilla tactics, initially targeting Soviet-dominated Europe.

Long before the Korean War, Colonel Bank had championed the idea of a specially trained guerrilla unit within the army. Fortunately, he found an ally in Brig. Gen. Robert McClure, head of the army's psychological warfare staff at the Pentagon. The outbreak of the Korean War further validated Bank's assessment, and Special Forces became part of a unit known as United Nations Partisan Forces Korea (UNPFK).

According to official Green Beret history sources, although 2,300 enlisted men and officers were authorized for the group at Fort Bragg, at the time of Colonel Bank's arrival only one warrant officer and eight enlisted men reported for duty. Eventually, a thousand men joined: combat veterans of World War II and Korea, ex-Rangers, airborne troopers, and former OSS officers—men like Lt. Col. Albert Scott Madding, who played a pivotal role in Special Forces history. Colonel Bank and his staff handpicked these soldiers from across the army, choosing them primarily for their receptiveness to and ability to learn all types of warfare.

One of Colonel Bank's first initiatives was to relocate the Psychological Warfare Center from Fort Riley, Kansas, to Fort Bragg. A number of other Special Forces members, including Colonel Madding and M. Sgt. Francis J. Ruddy, worked with him in this effort. The PWC at Fort Bragg not only offered specialized instruction in all phases of unconventional warfare but also served as an institution of higher learning for the research and conduct of counterinsurgency operations. The center subsequently evolved into the unconventional war headquarters for all United States military counterinsurgency efforts. Thanks to Colonel Bank, innumerable Special Forces operatives have acquired a new hometown in Fort Bragg, North Carolina—from which they have set out to change the course of history.

### On the Shoulders of Giants

In our initial orientation, we learned that the traditions of Special Forces dated back to 1942. But even then they were following in historic footprints.

Thus, before we could begin teaching counterinsurgency, we had to learn about the accomplishments of our remote predecessors. We were taught how Rogers's Rangers, named for their commander, Maj. Robert Rogers, stalked the enemy in woods and swamps during the French and Indian War. They were the first of America's unconventional forces.

The U.S. Army–Canadian First Special Services Forces, which originated on 2 July 1942, at Fort William Henry Harrison, Montana, played an active role in World War II. These units included the British and Canadian Commandos and the Devil's Brigade. Their approach to warfare developed its own momentum as they gained experience. The brigade saw most of its action in Italy and some action in France. Their specialty, close-quarters combat against numerically superior forces, was executed with great expertise and raw power.

We also learned about Darby's Rangers, the first ranger battalion under Maj. William O. Darby, formed on 19 June 1942, in Carrick Fergus, Ireland. The Rangers fought throughout Western Europe but staked their claim to fame when they scaled the cliffs of Pointe du Hoc as part of the D-Day invasion of Normandy. Their philosophy, as my old notes show, was simple: "Shock the enemy with quick strikes and deep thrusts leaving him paralyzed and confused."

In the Pacific, Lt. Gen. Walter Krueger had established a small elite force that he called the Alamo Scouts, after the historic fort in his hometown of San Antonio, Texas. In their eighty hazardous missions, they never lost a man in action. Perhaps their greatest feat was leading U.S. Rangers and Filipino guerrillas in an attack on a Japanese camp at Cabantuan. They freed all 511 allied prisoners. Although the Scouts never numbered more than seventy volunteers, they earned forty-four Silver Stars, thirty-three Bronze Stars, and four Soldiers Medals by the end of the war.

Besides these exceptional troops, a number of U.S. Army officers conducted guerrilla operations behind Japanese lines in the Philippines. Most notably, Colonel Volckmann escaped from the enemy and formed a Filipino guerrilla band in Northern Luzon that by 1945 consisted of five regiments. In addition, Maj. Wendell Fertig, a reservist, raised his own guerrilla force that ultimately totaled approximately twenty thousand fighters.

### "Wild Bill" Donovan and the OSS

Where even the Devil's Brigade and Darby's Rangers never ventured, a team of small parachuting units operated behind enemy lines in World War II, developing a network of contacts, giving instructions to local fighters, and waging guerrilla warfare on the enemy. Known unofficially as the Shadow Warriors, the team was a product of William Donovan, an imposing man-mountain of vision whose propensity for freewheeling activities had earned him the nickname "Wild Bill." His brand of special operations expanded the famous Civil War tactics of the Swamp Fox and Colonel Mosby into new techniques for airborne and guerrilla fighting. (A tough veteran of World War I, Donovan received the Medal of Honor for heroism on the Western Front in October 1918. We were also impressed by the fact that, in civilian life, he made a fortune as a Wall Street lawyer during the 1920s and 1930s.)

When World War II threatened to engulf the United States, Donovan convinced President Franklin D. Roosevelt of the need for a new type of organization, one that was capable of collecting intelligence and waging secret operations behind enemy lines. In 1941, President Roosevelt directed him to form an agency called the Coordinator of Intelligence (COI); and Donovan, who had been a civilian since World War I, became a colonel. Under his command, the agency blossomed quickly, forming operational sites in England, North America, India, Africa, Burma, and China. In 1942 it was renamed the Office of Strategic Services (OSS).

After the war, President Harry S. Truman disbanded the OSS, but not before its functions had achieved institutional status. Its awesome body of intelligence and operations experience, and a nucleus of experienced personnel, evolved into the Central Intelligence Agency on 18 September 1947.

Special Operations and Special Forces followed the OSS's guerrilla operatives as the United States faced yet another conflict, in Korea. In fact, Colonel Madding, commander of Special Forces when I arrived at Fort Bragg, had served with the CIA during the Korean War. He also served in World War II as a member of Merrill's Marauders of Burma, the title given to Col. Frank D. Merrill's 5307 Composite Unit. Colonel Madding told us in detail about many of his exploits.

The Marauders' three-thousand-man force staked out a piece of the Burmese jungle and dared the Japanese to challenge it. The Japanese accepted the challenge and lost to the Marauders in five major battles and seventeen skirmishes. However, the Marauders' greatest feat—the one that inspired us twenty or more years later, as we sloshed through the Asian jungles—was their miles-long march through the thick Burmese foliage en route to capturing an airfield at Myitkyina.

We spent many hours watching movies, discussing, and reading books about these legendary soldiers. We felt proud to have one of them, Colonel Madding, in our midst and honored to be continuing their legacy.

By now we understood that, for the U.S. Army, special operations were not new, and as trainers, we had to make sure that all upcoming trainees fully appreciated the courage and sacrifice of our predecessors. We truly were standing on the shoulders of giants. It was a place that I recognized, remembering my family's history and its perseverance in the face of adversity.

Armed with such inspiration, we of the 10th and 77th Special Forces developed a passion to capture the spirit and character of our predecessors and recreate it in our own times. Throughout the 1950s and early 1960s, with the evolution of the 10th, 77th, and 1st Special Forces Groups and the 14th Operational Detachment, we strove to pattern ourselves on those skilled and courageous men.

We soon realized, though, that our knowledge of actual operations was sketchy at best. The more we heard about our predecessors, the more we began to wonder how their exploits were accomplished. Certainly the essence of Special Forces was to meet the real and present challenge, to adapt to changing circumstances. Then we heard that Mao Tse-tung, first chairman of the People's Republic of China, had developed a new and shrewd brand of warfare that would require us to formulate innovative ways to cope with it—a rumor that proved to be true.

Another persistent rumor was that we were intended to build a Special Operations force that would work in conjunction with other nations' conventional armies. This rumor also proved to be substantially true. Still another rumor concerned the nature of guerrilla warfare itself. Guerrilla tactics, we understood, used subversives, insurgents, and assassins and fought primarily by ambush rather than traditional combat, and by infiltration rather than man-to-man combat. That is, we would be learning how to teach operatives to defeat enemy forces by eroding and exhausting them. However, it soon became clear that that rumor was only half right. There would be situations where it was mandatory to engage the enemy directly.

As rumors crystallized into common knowledge, we realized that in Special Forces we were conceived as multipliers and teachers first but would be expected to fight—ferociously and ingeniously—when necessary and be ready to serve at any moment and in any place.

As multipliers, we would be sent to train one basic unit, the battalion, in a given country for periods of six months. In a type of pyramid effect, that battalion would in turn train another. In other words, the training would "multiply" throughout the country's defense organizations.

Because the decision makers in Washington were not entirely sold on the proposed unconventional approach to warfare, our senior officers waged tremendous uphill battles to get us accepted as a workable and potentially effective force. Col. Edson D. Raff (who assumed command after Colonel Bank), Colonel Madding, Col. Donald C. O'Rourke, Master Sergeant Ruddy, SFC Fred Williamson, and the rest of us worked hard to get the training programs up and running quickly, so that we would be able to prove our value. Meanwhile, as we trained others, we were training ourselves.

### Training the Trainers

The A-team or detachment, which consisted of twelve to fourteen soldiers, was the basic unit of organization and operation for the Special Forces in 1952. A captain commanded the unit, with a lieutenant serving as the executive officer. There were ten enlisted men: one served as team sergeant, making it a traditional A-team. This configuration gave the team true self-sufficiency. We operated much like a family or clan and quickly discovered that a team of well-trained soldiers could live and operate as an independent unit under almost any conditions for indefinite periods.

At the time, an Operations Group was made up of FC (coordinating) detachments consisting of FA-teams with a control or headquarters unit (referred to as the FD-detachment or team) and basic administrative support personnel, less than three hundred men in all. (Now the count is around a thousand, with three battalions, a headquarters element, and a support organization.) The administrative team members were not, as my notes record it, an active part of operations. They did not deploy overseas in operational activities nor could they belong to functional teams elsewhere, although it was possible for them to join an operations team if selected and then qualified by training. (It appears that the designations FA, FC, FD, and other team classifications simply evolved into new and different meanings as we went along.)

During these early years, Special Forces enlisted personnel trained in five military occupational specialties. They included American and foreign weaponry, medical techniques, basic field and combat construction, radio and advanced communications, and intelligence gathering. These specialties encompassed all aspects of national and international warfare.

In training periods, we worked on becoming the specialized cadre for training allied militias in every military field, from basic weaponry to airborne operations. We trained primarily to form and lead resistance movements throughout any dominated region and to use unconventional techniques in case of total war.

By 1955, more than two years into our Special Forces training, we saw ourselves as a "new face of war."

We trained in twelve-member teams, and all team members were required to be cross-trained. Training activities took place throughout the world. In the United States, for a couple of months we trained in warfare techniques at Fort Bragg and Camp McCall, both in North Carolina. At Camp McCall, we spent some time on cold-weather maneuvers. However, the majority of cold-weather training was at the Mountain and Cold Weather Training Center high in the mountains surrounding Camps Hale and Carson, Colorado. At these bases, we learned the art of cross-country skiing and hiking in snow, and with this, we acquired high-altitude endurance. We also trained at the Wind River Indian Reservation in the Grand Tetons, Wyoming. Jungle warfare training was conducted in Panama.

In the Virgin Islands, we trained in scuba diving and underwater demolition, while the swamps near Camp Lejeune, North Carolina, served as the sites of numerous training exercises. Amphibious training, conducted several times a year at the Little Creek Amphibious Center base in Norfolk, Virginia, included beach landings, troop carrier, and submarine exercises. Here we were required to live on subs (a nightmare for me) and to undergo high-speed transport familiarization.

An early test of physical fitness was a two-mile, fifteen-minute run in heavy combat boots that truly bedeviled me at first. Later on it would look like a stroll in the park. As breathtakingly excruciating as our training was, as we pushed ourselves to the brink of exhaustion, we must have sensed what our leaders already knew: Under such circumstances our true characters would manifest. Those constant trials and tribulations were intended to test our endurance by breaking down our natural defenses. Qualifying for the Special Forces meant coping with unpredictable changes, against a daily routine of ever-lengthening cross-country treks, progressively heavier packs, and less and less sleep.

The magic number of weeks was fifty-two, the official qualifying period at the time. However, the torment was extended an additional week with a hundred-mile cross-country trek to Fort Bragg from Camp Lejeune, North Carolina. This was a five-day trip that I remember well.

During the week before the hike back to camp, we had completed a brutal survival exercise. Because of the dangerous circumstances, we trained in two-man teams. Devoid of food, shelter, or any of the other common necessities, this "staying alive" activity closely simulated the realities of the areas to which we would be deployed. Our only tools were a bayonet, a utility knife, and our wits. At times, I almost passed out from hunger, but overall I did all right—but even now, looking back, I do not understand how. As we sometimes say in the South, I "made do."

For the most part, we could only trap wild game, such as birds, snakes, fish, and rabbits, which became staples in our diet. We were instructed not to use our weapons, presumably to avoid shooting accidents, because even blanks—all we had in the way of ammunition—can kill within a certain range. (We did fire blanks into fishing coves on creeks and riverbanks. The repercussions from the discharge of the weapons stunned the fish, causing them to float to the top.) When available, we supplemented our diet of wild game and fish with mussels and clams. In addition, unofficially it was permissible to "borrow" chickens from farms. We "borrowed" quite a few.

During these maneuvers, we came upon an old deserted barn and farmhouse. Inside the house, we found old cornmeal grits, probably left there for years, that we soaked, made palatable with salt and pepper, and cooked. It was especially a treat for me, being from the South where grits is a food staple, although everybody ate heartily.

On the hundred-mile trek back to Fort Bragg from Camp Lejeune, we got two hot meals a day (all we wanted to eat) and the hope of being able to rest upon reaching our destination. An ambulance was on call during the entire trip. After almost a month of living off the land, I had lost all excess body fat; only thoughts of food and rest kept me going as we made our way back.

Throughout the training, the evaluation process continued to reveal those among us who could or could not fit into the Special Forces mold. Naturally, we assumed that some of us would fail—an assumption that proved to be accurate. Based upon evaluations from the training officers, senior NCOs, and other personnel who supervised, supported, or assisted us, a final evaluation board determined who would graduate. As well-trained conventional soldiers, we were also an active part of this evaluation and the special training of each other.

Among other items, these reports indicated trainees' attitude, ingenuity, knowledge, relationships with fellow team members, interactions with members of the training team, physical and mental health, and elation and enthusiasm for the training. In other words, the portfolio presented a comprehensive assessment of trainees' potential effectiveness for future missions in foreign countries. Slightly more than three-fourths of us completed the course. A close friend of mine washed out during the last week. I was more than surprised—no, *delighted*—to be among the survivors.

Nevertheless, the training did not end with the completion of these initial qualifications tests. Months of grueling field exercises were followed by extensive training in every kind of weapon and equipment imaginable. We trained in the proper use of 22-caliber, silencer-equipped pistols and a variety of grappling and rappelling gear. (So-called action movies have educated most civilians about how such equipment was intended to be used.)

Then, there were the "top secret" weapons handling and briefings sessions. Since we had to wear complete protective gear, we assumed the worst—possibly nuclear contamination—because by this time (1954) the wars of "national liberation" and the "liberation fronts" were in the common vocabulary. The French and the communists even referred to a third world war as a "revolutionary war." Although we were reluctant to use such terminology, the United States was also preoccupied with the threat of another world war and a potential nuclear holocaust.

International tensions about nuclear war proved to have a chilling effect on those of us who had made the grade. I began to wonder what I was doing there, because if nuclear war did break out, we would be training guerrilla fighters behind the lines. What would guerrilla warfare look like in the nuclear age? At Fort Bragg, many of us believed that we would prepare nuclear weapons to detonate after we left a country. I did not know exactly what to expect.

Meanwhile, since I didn't know whether or not I was training with real weapons, I assumed that the weapons we handled were radioactive. I also did not know what the effects of exposure to these weapons would be if this proved to be true. We all understood the predictable effects of a nuclear explosion near us, but what of mere contact in the field? Of the original sixteen members of 14th Detachment, three eventually succumbed to cancer. Exposed to radioactivity? It could be a normal statistic, but it still haunts me.

A combination of classroom instruction and practical application was a vital part of preparation for any mission. This was especially true for raid and ambush training. First, we spent an hour or so in the classroom; then, we went outside to rehearse what we learned. Usually an old building served as the objective. We would form one behind the other, usually from a ditch just out of sight, and rush the target.

I remember these drills as if they happened yesterday. A senior NCO acted as an enemy soldier lying face down on the ground. The storming team members ran to him and one trooper covered him while another team member turned him over to search for weapons. Simultaneously, a senior NCO or training officer would typically say, "Archer, we've got a problem." It was then incumbent upon me to use prior experiences and training to take whatever action was appropriate to ensure the mission's success. Somehow, I usually took the right action.

### The Invisible Hand

It was up to each of us, as Special Forces cadres, to determine our future ability to operate realistically in all military areas of responsibility, particularly human relations. Special Forces had established a reputation for devotion and determination long before we showed up. We knew that we would be operating behind enemy lines, under conditions in which survival was uncertain. While this challenge alone was enough for us to strive to become all we could be, we also acquired a sense of becoming part of a special group of top soldiers.

We knew Special Forces troopers were superior soldiers; still, it was hard to conceive of the awesome qualifications required of us. To survive, operate, teach, and influence military operations behind enemy lines, we had to operate with top security clearance and be totally efficient in all forms of warfare. These types of warfare included mountain, jungle, and underwater operations, demolition, usage of foreign weapons, and airborne techniques, enabling us to infiltrate enemy territories from the sea and air and by land. And we would do that as a team.

We focused intensely on the "spirit of being the best." Within the context of Special Forces evaluation, this meant, for example, being timely, precise and concentrating more on the task to be done than on the perceived anguish of doing it. To being the best, I added the "togetherness" program, as I called it, to the medical indoctrination at Smoke Bomb Hill during the so-called Prefix 3 training phase (the fifty-two-week qualification course). Its commentary became a part of our team's precourse reading.

Growing up in rural Mississippi, I learned the importance of knowing how to work with people at my father's knee. Cooperation was an essential tenet of the "Invisible Hand" theory that my family lived by. The theory is that there is a "felt" influence in a community that binds people together, keeping them close and safe in bad times, especially youth. Since this influence was real, direct, and "touched" us—albeit unseen—we termed it the Invisible Hand.

Ours was the kind of community that develops under stress from outside elements, and I saw a clear need to bring some of my family's wisdom to Special Forces training, which would lead us inevitably to dangerous and soul-challenging experiences. Basically, I tried to foster my father's attitude in our daily military activities.

My father had a powerful sense of community and, more importantly, of the *strength* of community—indeed, the survival value of our living, not each as one person focused only on his own interests, but as "one spoke in a wagon wheel." We were encouraged to make decisions together and to include the best interests of everyone in the choices we made as individuals. When we felt threatened by any force outside our own community, we could feel the reassuring presence of that bond and would know that the Invisible Hand would be there for us.

I knew that, whatever lay before us in Special Forces, we could not operate as "every man for himself." After six months of my appeals for some attention to the importance of personal cooperation during training, Capt. Harry G. Cramer, the operations and training officer, permitted me to introduce a brief "human side" to our Special Forces medical unit program. I was and am also grateful to M. Sgt. Francis J. Ruddy and S5 Earl Kalani, who were strong supporters of the course. They deserve a lot of credit for incorporating these ideas into our training.

Drawing upon my background and experience in personal survival during previous times, I used a host of other values to support my general thesis. The standard military education may not emphasize compassion, kindness, thoughtfulness, consideration, tenacity, resiliency, fortitude, integrity, loyalty, honor, courage, and commitment, to name a few—but for the very special challenges ahead of the Special Forces, I felt it was necessary to underscore such values.

Soon the concept permeated all aspects of our team training and the 77th Special Forces training activities, including the PSYOPS (psychological warfare) and Special Forces headquarters. The Invisible Hand's mandate of "all for one and one for all" become a part of our thinking. Its influence was quite evident later in Vietnam and other countries where we introduced and perpetuated the art of working together in counterinsurgency, and in the molding of various indigenous people into viable anti-communist forces.

Because we operated on our own, for the most part, missions demanded high motivation and total cooperation, in addition to technical proficiency. For us, the concept of the Invisible Hand became a superb model for success. I am still very proud of this contribution to the Special Forces effort.

### Medical Training: A Critical Specialty

All Special Forces troops at Fort Bragg participated in a thirty-eight-week course, primarily dealing with what to do to save lives in an actual war. The course was led by infantry and medical technicians who had experience as general and pathology paramedics, physician assistants, surgical technicians, nursing assistants, and practical nurses. These professionals came from diverse locations, including the Ranger and airborne schools at Fort Benning, Georgia. I had undergone similar training earlier in my military career in Chanute Field and at Fort Sam Houston.

I cannot overstate the importance of medical support to the threatened populations whom we assisted. We always had to be positive and assertive in our approach to medical training. We understood that part of our mission would be to help rectify any medical and nutritional problems of indigenous populations, wherever we were. Since the sick and wounded rarely received help from their own communities, we had to be able to identify local flora and fauna that had an impact on health, positive or negative.

Instead of a simple briefing, our medical sessions lasted from one to three hours. For conventional units, the lectures may have been tedious, but we knew that the knowledge was important for us; I listened very carefully.

Education about poisonous plants and infected or poisonous animals was one of the training's main elements. Snakes—identification of, treatment of bites of, avoidance of, and (not incidentally) cooking and consumption of—received due attention. The instructor, a veteran medic of the Korean War, lectured on a broad range of environmental hazards and explanations of the rather sophisticated ways that poisons and bacteria interact to create trauma. We learned recognition features of plants, effects from contact, control measures, medication options, and other details. We also learned that tea bags can be used to treat swollen, watery eyes resulting from sun blindness and other causes and that boiled pine needles are effective as a laxative.

We would be teaching the local people in various countries remedies for horse bites, ticks, and parasites. We spent a significant amount of time learning to recognize and treat diseases, identify the vectors of transmission, and assess the chances for survival once symptoms appeared. We were told how to deal with rabies, which was prevalent in Vietnam, Laos, Thailand, and other countries that the U.S. Army targeted for future Special Forces missions.

Coming from a rural background, I was no stranger to living off the land. While growing up back home, I was heir to my father's and aunt's legacy of laws of the outdoors. In turn, I was able to share my knowledge with my team members. How else would they have known that wild game tends to be lower in cholesterol and that raccoons, opossums, and frog legs are rich in protein?

For survival training in the United States, I was well equipped with woods lore. Beechnuts, hickory nuts, walnuts, and pine nuts, for example, are excellent sources of protein. Common weeds like burdock and its cousin, sheep sorrel, contain approximately 190 milligrams of Vitamin C, in boiled "poke salad" (a popular Southern dinnertime vegetable). Strawberry plant leaves can be prepared as a tea. Of course, accurate *positive* identification was the key to safe use of wild plants for food or medicine in any part of the world.

The final phase of medical instruction occurred in the animal laboratory under the close supervision of doctors. Our first commandment was to understand, accept, and practice the Special Forces medical creed, a type of Hippocratic Oath that describes the limits of our rights to perform medical services. In other words, the professionals constantly reminded of our status as specialists and professional soldiers, not doctors.

We learned operating room procedures, amputation, suturing, and general handling of wounds. We learned how to give our wounded dogs scrupulously compassionate care. Learning to alleviate their suffering enabled us to bring the same passion and dedication to handling the same vital functions for human beings, later in the field.

As team medic, my responsibility included overall entry-level training of future Special Forces personnel during missions. Therefore, when I completed the initial medical course at Fort Bragg, I attended the Medical Field Service School at Fort Sam Houston for advanced medical instruction. This phase of training included advanced emergency first aid; basic and regional human anatomy; basic human physiology; pharmaceutical calculations; basic medical technology; pharmacology I, II, and II; drug dosage; and therapy.

I made it through with flying colors—owing, at least in part, to other aspects of my military experience as well as mastering the medical training as such. I was a good medic. People skills and grace under pressure go a long way in the healing arts, and all of us were learning them, sometimes the hard way.

### Ready or Not . . .

A test came sooner than expected. I had gone out to purchase parachute boots, at the PX, directly across a narrow street from a mess hall. As I left the PX, I heard overhead the erratic sputtering of an aircraft in trouble. I figured that it was a troop carrier because earlier I noticed what appeared to be C-119 carriers passing over our area, apparently heading for an area drop zone.

Looking up, I saw the aircraft. For a moment, it appeared to be landing on top of the PX. My natural instinct to escape kicked in, and I sprinted to get out of its path. I did not know where I was trying to go—naturally I could not run as fast as the aircraft—so I attempted to zigzag my way to safety. I didn't see the wire stretched across the small lawn I was crossing in front of one of the barracks. It cut the flesh on my right shin to the bone. I still carry the scar as a reminder—but at the time I found more urgent matters to attend to.

The aircraft did not land on the PX but crashed into the mess hall instead. Huge clouds of smoke filled the air. Gathering my wits, I scrambled to my feet and headed toward the mess hall, bleeding leg and all, reaching it at about the same time as Sgt. Allen Maggio and SFC Antonio "Tony" Boggia. Another master sergeant and several other soldiers had also come to the rescue.

Fortunately, it was not mealtime. However, there were cooks and men on kitchen police duty in the building. Rushing into the mess section, we began to evacuate people, using chairs to lift fallen objects from some. For those able to move on their own, we showed them how to get outside. Others we dragged and carried to the exits.

Turning to the aircraft, we evacuated the crew. We did not let the eminent danger of an explosion from the leaking fuel tank deter us. In the tradition of Special Forces, we attempted to improvise by sealing the gas leak with available kitchen soap; it didn't work, but the feared explosion fortunately did not occur.

Regrettably, several lives were lost that day. Our emergency preparedness proved good, however, and the scar reminds me every day how much worse the results of the crash could have been. It could have been a major disaster had we not worked together so well.

### Airborne Training: Becoming "Jump Qualified"

To become a member of Special Forces or Special Forces Operations, we had to be airborne or "jump" qualified at Fort Benning, Georgia. Our training would lead us eventually to airborne operations.

In an airborne unit, even the cooks in garrison need to be jump qualified. Although Special Forces was not an airborne unit, as such, all enlisted personnel were assigned specialties at Fort Bragg that an airborne unit would require. Some medical units would not ordinarily be jumping out of aircraft, but my particular assignment as a medic gave me the option to attend airborne school.

Special Forces senior NCOs and commanders viewed airborne training from the perspective of how it could be used in the execution of missions. The possibility of forced entry behind enemy lines was one of the major reasons for requiring a Special Forces trooper to become airborne qualified. The tremendous prestige and pride associated with having earned the paratrooper insignia were added incentives for us all. We knew we would stand tall when we achieved it; we would stand *proud*.

To be successful in airborne school, the first question we asked ourselves was whether we had the right attitude to complete jump school—actually, the ability to focus so intensely on executing a task that we did not worry about inherent personal risks. (Years later, this attitude came to the forefront in countries when I was directly responsible for indigenous allies on a couple of jumps. And, although I knew the immediate danger, I had no conscious fear whatsoever.)

### Getting Fit to Jump

I will never forget the day of my arrival at Fort Benning's airborne school. They warned us. Our instructions said, "Soldiers at jump school must endure three weeks of intensive training"—the understatement of all time. We never walked, we ran. The actual run was called the "airborne shuffle."

First, we had to pass a rigid army medical examination that required us to meet the established physical fitness standards for a twenty-one-year-old. I was almost that young, so I had no problem passing the examination. But before I could say anything appropriate, like "Wow" or "Geronimo," I found myself up at five o'clock every morning for muscle-tearing physical training (PT), commonly referred to as the "Army dozen." This series of exercises included bend-and-reach, sit-ups, and running in place and more, followed by a brisk three-to-four-mile run.

I was so enthusiastic about jump school that I was up every morning at four-thirty to make certain that I was all set for the five o'clock reveille formation.

Running around Lee Field, the training area, we sang, "Airborne, airborne, have you heard? We're gonna jump from those great big birds." However, regardless of my enthusiasm, airborne training was the most physically punishing three weeks of my life. It outdistanced previous training, including basic, by a country mile. The weather was torrid. Fluids poured from my body. We were required to take salt pills. Every morning I thought that I would not make it through that day. Somehow I did.

One key to completing airborne training successfully is to approach it gradually, in a systematic manner. During the first week, we studied equipment and landing techniques. In addition, in order to qualify to participate in the second week of training, we had to make a jump from a thirty-four-foot tower while attached to a cable. Without a doubt, those thirty-four feet were the longest feet that anyone could imagine. I felt as if I were jumping off the Empire State Building.

During the second week, we wore the T-7 parachute, which the army had been using since World War II. Attached to a cable that lifted us 250 feet above the ground, we dangled in midair before being released to float to the ground under a pre-inflated canopy (not the T-7 parachute, which we wore only to become accustomed to the weight). Although the risks were minimal, soldiers occasionally injured themselves when they became entangled in the cables. Luckily, I never did.

### "Go!"

During the third week, we made five exits from high-performance C-124 and C-119 aircraft. We also learned the technique of individual free-fall and how to manually activate our parachutes.

Most of us jumped from the C-119. According to draftsman's calculations, as the story went around, it was impossible for a C-119 to fly. We laughed and told ourselves that a bumblebee theoretically can't fly, either, but it's a flying son-of-a-gun, right? Still, I did not find one iota of solace at the time in that similar bit of information about the C-119.

After two weeks of torturous training, I found myself airborne and facing the decisive moment—we were going to jump. From my position halfway down the stick of jumping (meaning I was halfway down the line of soldiers preparing to exit the aircraft), I looked from the front door down to the ground—twelve hundred feet below. I knew what was coming because we had learned a lineup cadence to help us remember the jumpmaster's sequence of orders: "Stand up, hook up, shuffle to the door. Step right out and count to four."

Shortly, I found myself at the head of the line and, as if on cue, the jumpmaster, a corporal, yelled, "Get ready!"

My stomach knotted up.

Then he commanded, "Hook up!" The blood drained from my fingers as I hooked my static line to the cable.

"Stand in the door!" he shouted.

I froze momentarily.

"Go!"

It is probably just as well that I cannot recall my exact words—spoken or unspoken—at that point.

As I exited the aircraft, the propeller blast sent me hurling through the air.

The anchor line—the cable, or "lifeline" as we called it—ran the length of the aircraft. Upon a count of "hup . . . one thousand, hup . . . two thousand, hup . . . three thousand, hup. . . four thousand," the static line played out. Its sudden jerk pulled the parachute out of my backpack and it opened. The T-7 had a terrific opening shock.

"What the hell am I doing here?" I wondered aloud.

However, as I looked overheard and saw the C-119 speeding away, I became elated. "Heck, here I am out of the aircraft. There it goes and I am floating down to the ground. It can't be too bad from here on."

For the next few seconds, I remained on an adrenaline high. Four seconds later, after descending twelve hundred feet at the rate of eighteen to twenty feet per second, I hit the ground safely. I landed on the balls of my feet, followed by ground contact of the calf, thigh, buttocks, and back of my shoulders, respectively—all according to the PLF, the parachute landing fall we had been trained for.

There was a saying at jump school that anyone who said he wasn't nervous during an airborne operation was either a liar or dangerous. Even so, I was not particularly afraid during the approximately 110 parachute jumps that I made. When I stepped out of an aircraft, I would feel stunned as the cold air hit my face, and I felt briefly as though I were being thrown toward the ground. After the parachute began to open, though, I would regain control of my senses—and then was too busy to think about being afraid.

To describe the experience of jumping, imagine stepping out into pitch darkness carrying one hundred and fifty pounds of equipment and falling eight hundred or more feet onto a cold, wet drop zone. This was the first step. To me, the fun part was that we were just getting started and soon would have the privilege of repeating the process. This is probably not the average person's idea of fun.

After three jumps, we received more equipment to carry, with additional pieces added on each successive jump. This stepped-up training wiped out a large number of the trainees, although I do not recall any of them being from Fort Bragg.

To get ready for the next level of training, to become jumpmasters, we were required to make at least three additional jumps and complete another challenging leadership course. Once qualified as a jumpmaster, it became incumbent upon each of us to ensure that fellow paratroopers safely exited the aircraft during training exercises and in combat or other Special Forces operations. We were then qualified to serve as aircraft commanders.

Despite taking precautions, accidents and injuries did happen. The injuries sustained by this group of trainees were not due to parachute malfunction. The problems resulted from troopers' getting entangled in the risers or lines. Initially, we would stand in the aircraft doorway with our hands positioned on each side. Then, we would jump up and out about thirty-six inches. This procedure posed a serious safety risk.

It was difficult to execute that move when an aircraft was in flight, especially the C-123 and C-130, both of which had extremely high propeller blasts. Excessive turning upon exit may have caused the twisting and tumbling into the opened parachute that led to injuries. Later, the procedure changed to walking straight out the door at a 45-degree angle.

Most injuries were impact injuries—soreness, broken legs, sprained ankles and knees. In fact, we called aspirin "the airborne soldier's friend," "a Special Forces friend," and pain relievers our "airborne candy."

Nevertheless, any airborne soldier will tell you that the pain, risks, and injuries are worth the privilege of wearing the airborne wings. Why? Probably not for the money; at that time a jump-qualified, enlisted Special

Forces soldier earned only $55 more per month. Officers received twice as much. (Eventually, in the late 1950s, these amounts became $110 and $220, respectively.)

Within the Special Forces, as in any military community, rank insignia drew respect. Within the airborne and Special Forces communities, the airborne wings signified a special type of achievement. At Fort Benning, the airborne community took pride in awarding the wings. I won my novice airborne wings at Fort Benning, for the five static-line jumps.

Later I would qualify for Master Wings—a star with a wreath around the wings—for sixty-five jumps, twenty-five combat equipment jumps, four night jumps, five mass technical jumps, service with an airborne unit for at least thirty-six months, and completion of a jumpmaster course according to army regulations. (Another wings award, Senior wings with a star, was earned by thirty jumps, fifteen combat equipment jumps, two night jumps, and two mass technical jumps, plus completion of a jumpmaster course, an advanced course in airborne training, and at least two years of service with an airborne unit.)

Jump wings with a combat star signified that the paratrooper had jumped in combat. From a distance, it looked like a mustard stain. Every soldier, Special Forces or regular, wanted it. Any soldier—novice, senior, or master—could wear the combat star.

### Putting Airborne Training into Practice

Because of the immediacy of our missions, we maintained our proficiency by jumping on average every four to six weeks. Most of these jumps were at night and in full combat gear.

Night jumps are a totally awesome experience. All of a sudden, the sky gets extremely quiet. You look up and see the aircraft flying away. The only sound you hear is the beating of your own heart. Once you gain your bearings, you look around to ensure that no other parachute is in your glide path. You lower your equipment and pack to the end of a lowering line. Then, you smile and say "Airborne!"

At one time, we held an unofficial ritual, similar to hazing in college fraternities, not inaccurately dubbed the Blood Wings Ceremony by shocked civilians who heard about it. For us, it signified the official end to the training of the airborne trooper. It also introduced us to our subsequent initiation into a special clan of full-fledged parachutists. The wings were placed on the initiate's bare chest. Then, a fellow parachutist (someone with a powerful arm) would batter them deeply into his flesh in an attempt to make them stick.

I understand that "Blood Wings" initiation no longer takes place. The reason for ending it was that such rituals supposedly detract from a soldier's dignity. Nevertheless, in earlier days we considered it a bonding experience. It made me feel like a part of the "big, bad paratroopers."

### International Training: The Lodge Bill Soldiers

Fort Bragg trained not only U.S. troops but also many from friendly foreign countries. During the mid-1950s, a number of East Europeans joined the classes of the 10th and the 77th Special Forces. They had escaped communist terror in their own countries—Poland, China, and Czechoslovakia, to name a few. Congress passed a measure in mid-1950, introduced by Henry Cabot Lodge, which allowed these people to join the U.S. Army. We respectfully referred to them as "Lodge Bill" soldiers. They trained along with us, learning comprehensive aspects of Special Forces. More often than not, they participated in the entire training program, including airborne training.

The United States and the Special Forces planned for this group to evolve into a regiment of twenty-five hundred troops (half Europeans and half native-born Americans). Their primary function was to conduct Special Forces missions behind the lines in their homelands. In return for five years of such military service, they became United States citizens.

Training the Lodge Bill soldiers proved to be a smart move on the part of the United States government. During the years that followed, when mostly indigenous people sponsored Special Forces in foreign countries, their ability to "fit in" was a valuable asset. Since they knew the people, territory, pulse, and language (of course they spoke with no trace of a foreign accent), they were able to serve us as supporters, trainers, and advisors.

### Fit to Serve

Those of us who survived the training became the 10th Special Forces Group. We were in great physical shape, robust and versatile. Nevertheless, what we possessed went well beyond physical agility or the mastery of Special Forces concepts. The training fostered a sense of trust and teamwork that often spilled over into our leisure activities. These concepts are still important in my life after more than forty-five years. "Once a Special Forces soldier, always a Special Forces soldier" is still true.

Our outstanding athletics program boasted of soldiers who excelled in a broad spectrum of sports including football, basketball, and baseball. Although I would like to say that I was one of them, I cannot claim this honor. However, I was captain of the small bow and rifle teams and came to be quite proficient with them. They were my passion.

Indeed, basic Special Forces training proved to be one of my most interesting, exciting, challenging, and rigorous efforts, though this training proved much less physical than mental. I kept in top physical shape. Now, when anyone asks me why our missions were such successes, I immediately recall the values and leadership that the Psychological Warfare Center instilled in us. They were the factors that brought our tremendous potential to fruition.

### Visiting Home

Throughout my Special Forces training, thoughts of family were never far from my mind. I wanted to learn as much as I could, and not let the family down. It was important to me never to diminish my family's reputation for always striving to be the best. On leave after the last fifty-two weeks of formal training, I let my family know that the army was now my "other" family. I liked being an airborne trooper. I liked being a soldier. I liked being a special part of the service. I was young and certainly gung-ho. After all, I was Special Forces qualified.

While home, it rained constantly, for several days providing a "mist opportunity" for Papa and me. Some people may have been dreading the rain—floods are always a threat in Mississippi—but Papa welcomed it. "I know that things are getting what they need," he told me. In dry, clear weather, he would have had less time for me. All the growing things were getting water that they needed, and Papa was getting a chance to absorb some of his son's experiences.

The wet weather gave us a chance to discuss many things regarding military operations. We discussed how the military concept relates to the family, the community, and the world. We talked about the importance of maintaining solid, old-fashioned values and traditions, such as trust, loyalty, honesty, and teamwork.

Ivy Land, a ninety-something-year-old relative, joined us one day, and backed up Papa's point of view. "We've always lived that way," he told me. I already knew that I always would.

### "I Am an American Special Forces Soldier. . . ."

Between 1952 and 1954, we continually proved ourselves in a multitude of stressful situations. Even during the most difficult of days, I felt great confidence that I would make it big. In moments of doubt—and there were some—I could still count on the "promises," the potentials my life held, because I had been taught to believe in them. My mother taught me that a potential for greatness is a birthright of everyone. Every influence of my community and family had taught me, from childhood, that given the right conditions, I could do anything. When I came to Fort Bragg to be molded into a Special Forces operative, I knew the right conditions were at hand. And when the time came, I was proud to take the oath of the Special Forces—and ready to serve.

### SPECIAL FORCES CREED

I am an American Special Forces soldier. A professional, I will do all that my nation requires of me.

I am a volunteer, knowing well the hazards of my profession.

I will serve with the memory of those who have gone before me, Rogers' Rangers, Francis Marion, Mosby's Rangers, the first Special Forces and Ranger Battalions of World War II, the Airborne Ranger companies of Korea.

I am a professional soldier. I will teach and fight wherever my nation requires. I will strive always to excel in every art and artifice of war.

I know that I am called upon to perform tasks in isolation far from familiar faces and voices with the help and guidance of my God.

I will keep my mind and body clean, alert and strong, for this is my debt to those who depend upon me.

I will not fail those with whom I serve. I will not bring shame upon myself or the forces.

I will maintain myself, my arms, and my equipment in an immaculate state that befits a Special Forces soldier.

I will never surrender though I be the last. If I am taken, I pray that I will have the strength to spit upon my enemy.

My goal is to succeed in any mission and live to succeed again.

I am a member of my nation's chosen soldiery. God grant that I may not be found wanting, that I will not fail in this sacred trust.

As our creed declares, Special Forces breeds a level of confidence—a level of "never surrender." The time spent with Special Forces helped an ordinary person like me do extraordinary things.

## 2  *HAWAII, 1956*

### Prelude to Southeast Asia

By the time I arrived at Fort Bragg for training, the prime focus of Special Forces had shifted from Europe to Southeast Asia. Under the command of the Psychological Warfare Center, larger and larger numbers of Special Forces personnel had already been preparing for assignment as military teachers throughout the world. Since 1953, teams had been training to operate in Taiwan, Korea, Thailand, and what was then called French Indochina (now Vietnam, Cambodia, and Laos).

The fall of Dien Bien Phu was still in the future, but France was losing French Indochina. Insurgent groups demanding an end to colonial rule, some communist, some not, would soon drive them out, despite millions in U.S. aid.

In the fifties, the Cold War and the threat of nuclear annihilation drove the policy decisions of the major powers. The so-called domino effect, by which the loss of one small country to communism would lead to the loss of the next until the Red scourge engulfed Western civilization, looked like a real possibility to U.S. leaders, civilian and military. The power of post–World War II nationalist uprisings in the prewar colonies of European nations was secondary to the communist threat—even when they were the same thing.

Onto this scene of changing world events, we emerged—the army's newly formed unit, the 14th Special Forces Operational Detachment (Airborne) (Area), cadre of the 1st Special Forces Group (Airborne).

By the time we had completed our training, the French would have lost Vietnam at Dien Bien Phu (7 May 1954) and the Geneva Accords would have split the country in two, promising elections in two years that would never, in fact, take place. In 1955 Ngo Dinh Diem became president of a

Republic of South Vietnam so riven with factional strife—Buddhist, Cao Dai, Hoa Hao, Binh Xuyen, Montagnard, and, pervasively, communist Viet Minh—that a second Vietnam War was inevitable.

How would that war be fought, and by whom? What part would we play? We would soon find out.

### Airborne Proud and Looking the Part

The 14th had become one of most elite units in the U.S. Army after training at various locations, at Fort Bragg and elsewhere. A sixteen-man detachment, our team was commanded by a lieutenant colonel; the executive officer (XO), a major; and the operational officer (OR), a captain. A master sergeant, the senior enlisted man who supervised day-to-day operations, twelve senior sergeants, and one regular sergeant made up the remainder of the unit. Because of our mission and the identity of the people who made up this unit, an aura of secrecy shrouded us, even at Fort Bragg, at our remote Smoke Bomb Hill.

Prepared to be HALO (high-altitude, low-opening) paratroopers, scuba divers, mountaineers, and skiers, we were entering a different kind of war. Conventional warfare had *not* worked for the French. We would need flexibility and resourcefulness to combat the guerrilla warriors who had erased French Indochina from the map and now were expanding within divided Vietnam and her highly unstable neighbors. We were going to earn our place in history.

The 14th's first and only commander was Lt. Col. Albert Scott Madding. Two years earlier, he had served as deputy commander of the 10th Special Forces Group, operating in Germany (East and West). The segment dispatched to Germany had retained the name 10th Special Forces, while the one remaining at Fort Bragg was officially restructured and renamed the 77th Special Forces Group, Airborne.

The Pentagon had handpicked us from dossiers submitted by the Psychological Warfare Center at Fort Bragg. Colonel Madding and Capt. Harry Cramer, our operations and training officer, recommended me. We all knew that selection was an acknowledgment of our skills and character as officers and enlisted men. Every one of us knew we had some enormous challenges ahead of us, and our pride in being chosen was proportionate.

Our attitude about our apparel expressed some of that prideful spirit. We cherished our Corcoran jump boots, an important symbol of being airborne, and kept them spit-shined to the point where you could literally tie your necktie while looking into the toe or heel. (I once even had a pair of shined boots featured in a military publication.) We threatened any non-airborne soldier who bloused his boots with drastic vengeance. Our garrison cap (overseas) was cocked forward until it touched the forehead. There was no mistaking us for anybody else's group.

About this time, the quartermaster general of the army approved the maroon-and-green background for the parachute wings, the definitive symbol of being "airborne." The 77th Special Forces Group, Airborne, crest (teal blue with a yellow sinister running through it) was worn under the wings on the left side of our chest. The three arrows in the upper left-hand corner reflect the three methods of entry and exit from the operations area—by air, sea, and land. A globe in the bottom right-hand corner represents the global aspect of Special Forces operations. The group's motto, inscribed at the bottom, and the eagle surrounding the crest represent eternal vigilance, the watchword of a Special Forces unit.

We were definitely the "proudest of the airborne proud."

### "Killer Paratroopers"

In June of 1956, within two years of becoming operational, the 14th went to Hawaii. Local newspapers ran stories about our suspected missions to Vietnam and Thailand, speculating in print. "Killer Army Paratroops Will Make Jumps over Oahu," and "Foreign Government Places Bounty on Special Forces" blared the headlines.

All missions in which I participated, with the exception of the 1961 mission to Laos, engaged members from the 14th Special Forces Detachment (Area) (Airborne). The original 14th consisted, besides me, of Albert Scott Manning, Donald C. O'Rourke, Harry G. Cramer, Henry S. Furst, Raymond E. LaBombard, Donald C. Reynolds, Francis J. Ruddy, Robert L. Voss, Fred R. Williamson, Robert L. Bennett, Bobby A. Newman, Lester G. Ruper, Donald E. Stetson, and Earl Kalani. Michael Marano joined the unit later.

Rumors abounded; we heard that Vietnamese radio broadcasts reported bounties on Col. Madding, Major O'Rourke, Captain Cramer, and each enlisted man. However, nobody was trembling with dread. There were no shudders at this point. There were no premonitions of the countless deaths soon to occur in Vietnam. Certainly, we were highly interested in what might happen next, but we were not fearful or anxious. We knew what we had to do.

Aside from the rumors concerning the prices on our heads, what we enjoyed least about Hawaii was being "under the gun" constantly. Generally, we accepted that on the mainland the high command and staff did not see anything unique about Ho Chi Minh's war. As far as most of the senior leaders were concerned, conventional training—basic, leadership, organizational principles, tactics, and strategy—which had won America's wars in the past, would be more than adequate for Indochina.

Sadly, the concepts of Special Warfare and Special Forces met with harsh ridicule from the regulars. Unfortunately, too, it seemed that Washington was completely unaware of what we knew so well—that success against guerrilla warfare was unlikely without support from the people of the country in which it was happening. If only those "in authority" had realized that the front line of defense against paramilitary aggression had to be directed to the minds and hearts of the people—the threatened population—history might not read as it does now.

Mao Tse-tung had already demonstrated the principle repeatedly during his ten-thousand-mile "Long March" across China as he fled before Chiang Kai-shek's conventional forces. It was clear, to anyone who wanted to see it, that warfare was changing.

To gain popular support, Mao Tse-tung implemented codes of behavior designed to make the peasant feel that the Red Army was friendly and benevolent. Chiang Kai-shek's conventional forces had their own sort of relationships, not based on courtesy or conciliation. It should have been easy for the Pentagon to see why popularity would begin to snowball toward the irregulars who lived by the rules prescribed by Mao Tse-tung.

Although our leaders seemed indifferent to it, the USSR seemed to be very interested in special warfare. In 1956 the Soviet Union understood that "wars of national liberation" had to be fought by guerrillas and by infiltration, instead of through direct aggression. Guerrillas act when the risks are small and when physical and psychological effects on their enemies are greatest. They wage a war of erosion and exhaustion, and by assassination and ambush. It appeared to us that although Soviet troops continued to practice direct combat, they were making strides with their new war where the United States was falling behind.

We of the 14th Operational Detachment, paratroopers all, were prepared to fight the new war. We couldn't stay long enough to enjoy the beaches or Hawaiian hospitality. Indochina beckoned.

### "The Fish and the Sea"

Our Southeast Asia operation had begun in earnest earlier at Fort Bragg, with the return of Col. Madding and the operations officer from a top-level Pentagon meeting. Accompanied by Colonel Raff, they had proceeded to formulate plans for us to operate internationally from a base in Hawaii. As a senior Special Forces type of group, the 14th was to serve as a basic unit, the fundamental building block for all future operations in the Far East.

As a behind-the-enemy-lines guerrilla training unit, we were considered an alternative to full-scale war and were destined to become the first and (for a long time) only American combat-type unit in Vietnam. Our mission was to start a process that could help to bring peace and stability to Vietnam. Our assignment: to seek out, train, and support men capable of becoming effective guerrillas in Vietnam, and to seek out, engage, and counter unfriendly rebels throughout Southeast Asia. The focus was Vietnam, but we would see much of other countries in the area before arriving there.

We also inherited the official mission from our parent unit, the 77th Special Forces. My notes remind me that this was "to infiltrate by land, sea or air, deep into enemy-held territory and coordinate the resistance or guerrilla potential to conduct Special Forces operations, with emphasis on guerrilla clashes."

Even during basic infantry training, I understood that the purpose of special operations was to always be the result of direct intentions, sincere efforts, intelligent directions, and skillful execution. Success would depend on quick decisions in unfamiliar situations, choosing from numerous approaches. We felt ourselves to be among the toughest fighters and the most efficient trainers in the world, and now we would get to prove it.

From our study of the airborne infantry and the history of the paratroopers, we learned much about resistance, counteraction, and guerrilla fighting at Fort Bragg. Once we knew where we were going, we read whatever was available in print about special operations. I even made a special run on the Pentagon bookstore. Our reading covered the British experience in Malaysia and elsewhere, the French experience in Algeria and Vietnam, and anything else pertinent to putting down insurgencies. The writings of Mao were always handy.

In particular, we discussed Mao's metaphor of the "fish and the sea" — his reference to guerrillas' need for support. We reviewed with renewed interest Edgar Snow's book, *Red Star over China* (New York: Grove/Atlantic, 1989). That book gave us a firsthand account of the emphasis that both Mao Tse-tung and other experts placed upon good discipline and troop behavior as means of gaining popular support for a struggling revolutionary army.

*Red Star over China*, originally published in 1939, describes how rules for troop discipline were set to music and sung daily as an official Red Army song. Six of the rules that seemed to bring magical results were:

There shall be no confrontation whatsoever with the poor peasantry.

If you borrow anything, return it.

Replace all articles you damage.

Pay for everything that you purchase.

Be honest in all transactions with the peasants.

Be courteous and polite to the people and help them whenever you can.

These courtesies and others would make the common people feel that Mao's troops were friendly and benevolent and that the people's well-being was their top priority. In other words, the troops were being taught a lesson we would learn too: *Treat the people right, because they hold our lives in their hands.* The Special Forces were first taught this lesson formally and later put it into action as a principle of war. (In retrospect, I believe one reason for our country's failures in Vietnam was that some of our conventional troops failed to follow these simple rules.)

Indoctrination regarding Vietnam began in February 1955 as a sort of philosophical treatise pointing up the more covert and clandestine operations that we would encounter throughout Indochina. For that matter, it outlined a set of conditions found throughout the world. Regardless of country, the "national liberation" struggles shared several characteristics:

1. A native people dissatisfied with the existing form of government;

2. Often extreme hardship suffered by a substantial part of the population; and,

3. Sponsorship or support from the communists.

This was a "real" education in highly irregular warfare, or "front-line" warfare, which for us was largely untested. From where we stood it looked radically different from our usual area studies and briefings.

At least in theory, then, the 14th Special Forces Operational Detachment (Abn) (Area) was well prepared for Mao Tse-tung's insidious brand of war. We made preparations along new lines. Our initiatives aimed to build a force to fight in areas where conventional armies were incapable of operating and in ways that conventional armies couldn't even consider.

### The Controversial Green Beret: A Presidential OK

Special Forces had not yet become distinguished by the Green Beret headgear, but we would soon be. The regulation in effect at the time was AR 600-32, Uniform for Male Personnel and Special Regulation (SR) 600-32-1, Articles and Types of Uniforms for Male Personnel. However, our unit commanders had almost complete leeway regarding what we wore.

As members of the 10th and 77th Special Forces Groups, we began wearing the beret occasionally during field maneuvers at Fort Bragg. At the time, it was simply part of a wide assortment of odd headgear that we wore to distinguish ourselves from the ordinary soldiers. (Regular troops were restricted to wearing issue caps during training.) Sometimes we wore civilian clothes, and sometimes we wore a mixture of uniforms and civilian clothes. During exercises, we wore whatever was comfortable and allowed us to look like a partisan or possibly an insurgent. We simply wore anything odd.

Col. Jack T. Shannon, deputy commander, restricted the beret to field operations. Although instructed not to wear it with our dress uniform, I can tell you now that we disobeyed that instruction. After successfully harassing conventional troops on FTXs (field exercises), we would wear the beret downtown and dare anyone to try to prevent us from doing so. About 1954, we learned that even Col. William Ekman, commanding officer of the 10th Special Forces in Germany, approved the wearing of the green beret in Europe and that Special Forces troopers considered it a treasured part of their uniform. Word spread quickly and soon other units and civilians began to associate the beret with us.

While the debate over the Green Beret raged on, the Special Forces got its own official sleeve insignia. In August 1955 Lt. Col. O'Rourke and I served on a committee led by Capt. John W. Frye that designed an arrowhead-shaped patch containing an upturned dagger crossed by three lightning bolts. The shape of the arrowhead connects the Special Forces to its Native American heritage.

The dagger is characteristic of the World War II–era Devil's Brigade, 1st Special Services Force, our predecessors. The three lightning bolts represent the Special Forces ability to infiltrate by air, sea, or land. The teal blue color is the traditional color of U.S. Army unassigned units that symbolized the fact that the Special Forces belonged to no particular branch of the army but, rather, included personnel from all areas. Later, the black and gold airborne tab showing actual paratrooper capability came to highlight the paratrooper qualification of all assigned Special Forces troops.

The first real effort to get the Green Beret approved on an army-wide basis was spearheaded years later by Col. Edson Dungan Raff, head of the Psychological Warfare Center. Raff was a colorful, highly decorated World War II combat veteran, rumored to be a friend of President Eisenhower, who praised him highly. For some reason, unknown to us, the army's high-ranking authorities repeatedly rebuffed his attempts to make it official.

As in the case of the sleeve insignia, Colonel O'Rourke and I served on the committee that made recommendation regarding the Green Beret's crest. Its original crest was a silver Trojan horse worn on the left side above the ear. While accepting the sleeve insignia, conventional army generals still passionately objected to the dashing headgear and issued special orders against wearing it.

Later, however, we had an ally in President John F. Kennedy, who had always expressed strong faith in special warfare as an effective foreign policy tool, a proven entity. He called the Special Forces his "counterinsurgency warriors." We heard that Brig. Gen. William P. Yarborough had met the president, who threw his full support directly behind the adoption of the headgear.

In an earlier declaration from the White House, the president said this about the beret: "A symbol of excellence, a badge of courage, a mark of distinction in the fight for freedom." Subsequently, on 10 December 1961 the army designated the Green Beret as the official headgear for the Special Forces, although by that time we had already been wearing it for almost a decade!

Some years after the 14th came into existence, a Green Beret returned to President Kennedy under almost unthinkable circumstances. The president's family requested that Special Forces men form the honor guard at his burial in Arlington National Cemetery. When the ceremony concluded, Sgt. Maj. Francis J. Ruddy sadly took the beret from his head and placed it on our commander in chief's grave, along with the hats of the army, navy, and air force. To this day Special Forces soldiers ensure that a fresh Green Beret always lies above the president who loved and respected us as tough and highly competent guerrilla fighters.

We never forgot President Kennedy's admonitions in his earlier message approving the Green Beret, where he exhorted us to ". . . wear the beret proudly. It will be a mark of distinction and a badge of courage in the difficult years ahead." Indeed, it has been—and by then it had already established its traditions, in the jungles of Southeast Asia.

Our first mission from Fort Shafter, Hawaii, was to Thailand.

Earlier in 1956, after completing operational training at the 77th Special Forces Group (Abn) (Area), we received the mandate to operate throughout Asia. This decree specifically pertained to Southeast Asia and the South Pacific. We spent more than three months preparing for Thailand, under orders of strict secrecy. However, the elaborate precautions to disguise the mission and us did not fool anyone, except possibly the American public. According to some reports, Vientiane, Hanoi, Moscow, Peking, Paris, and other scattered spots not only knew that we were in Hawaii but also had our names and army serial numbers.

We were sent to Thailand before beginning operations in Vietnam. As the 14th Special Forces Operational Detachment (Abn) (Area), under the command of Colonel Madding, we were the first Special Forces unit committed to Thailand. We would be working with the Royal Thai Army.

Senior members of the team included Maj. Donald C. ("Paddy" or "Shorty") O'Rourke, Sgt. Maj. Francis J. Ruddy, M. Sgt. Henry Furst, SFC Everett C. White, and me.

The flight took off in June 1956. Traveling by C-123 aircraft, we parachuted directly into the initial training area at Trang, located approximately six hundred miles from Thai headquarters near the Malaysian border. In full operational gear, we were ready for anything. Although we were "dropping in" on a friendly country, we could easily see the advantages of entering less hospitable places in the area by parachute. Parachuting is fast; we could easily have bypassed any ground defenses that might have been in place during a hot war.

The next few hours we made final checks of our equipment. Every piece of gear was assigned to a team member and noted. We knew exactly who had what, so that in the event of actual combat we could find what we needed.

At about 2230 hours, we took off from Trang, headed for Lopburi, the nearest settlement. Through a scattered layer of clouds, we leveled off at a terrain hugging about six hundred feet, the height of jumps during combat. Troopers usually jump from twelve hundred feet.

We knew that Thailand faced many enemies both internally and externally. Insurgencies, incursions, banditry, and artillery fire occurred on Thailand's borders. While I felt that the jury was still out on President Eisenhower's so-called domino effect, it appeared to be quite visible in Southeast Asia.

Ironically, it also seemed that, although we had a distinct legacy of commitment in Asia and in Thailand at the time, few people cared. We did. As a unit, reflecting the larger Special Forces, the 14th cared about the possible domino effect, and we wanted to help countries, particularly Thailand, survive it.

### The Country and Its People

Soon after our arrival we began our orientation briefings to learn about Thailand.

Colonel Madding assigned me the task of briefing the team on the economy, culture, and traditions of the Thai people. The Thai government supplied all of the literature that I used in the session. However, I enjoyed being able to convey some favorite lessons that I had brought from home about appreciating the differences between people. Respect for the rights, property, opinions, ideas, and feelings of others works in any context. Bottom line: Treat all people with dignity regardless of your relationship with them.

The Thais were (and are) a sober, modest people with a great deal of national pride. They greatly respected all aspects of their country's culture. So, one of my first instructions to the team was to stand when we heard the national anthem, usually played on Thai military bases at 0800 hours and 1600 hours each day.

Another point was to show respect for the Thai religion. One symbol of such respect was to remove our shoes and behave soberly when entering Buddhist temples and to show respect for Buddhist statues, which the Thais considered sacred.

I reminded the team that, despite Bangkok's reputation as a "sin capital" during those times, native Thai women, in general, were extremely modest in dress and behavior. I cautioned the team that we, too, must dress modestly. We were not to go shirtless. We were to wear long pants—no shorts—on the streets, and beach attire on the beach only. Nude sunbathing on the beaches was illegal, although the average Thai was too polite to say so.

Clothing even played a role in certain religious observances. For instance, the literature recommended that we wear wash-and-wear clothing during the Buddhist New Year when tradition called for throwing water on anyone who passes by, a practice that the Thais rigidly adhered to.

All that was reasonable enough, but there were finer points as well. For instance, sitting in any position with one's feet pointed at anyone was taboo. This was much emphasized in literature provided by the government. Another taboo was touching the head. You do not touch the heads of Thais, not even children. (I once forgot my own teaching and touched the head of a young boy. Although neither the child nor the adults present showed any kind of reaction, a native friend later warned me that touching the child's head had been a serious social error.)

Moving on to less sensitive subjects, I briefed the group on Thailand's ways of doing business, explaining the country's transportation system. The railroad was the most important part of it. A network of tracks came out of Bangkok, extending all the way to our location at Lopburi and running as far as Chiang Mai and south to the frontier of Malaysia. Our unit would be using the system extensively. We could catch a train and go wherever we needed to go.

"Don't take candy from strangers," a familiar warning to children back in the States, took on new meaning in Thailand, especially on the trains and buses in Chiang Mai. The government sent us explicit instructions regarding the inherent dangers of doing so. Marijuana, hashish, opium, and other illegal drugs were readily available. A common practice was for dealers to report buyers to the police for a reward after making a sale. The Thais did prosecute foreigners. They still do.

I warned the team about the many con games in Bangkok, some of which included Westerners posing as tourists or dealers selling fake gemstones.

Even certain foods were subject to government warnings. We were cautioned against eating bananas because some varieties contained large, hard, tooth-cracking seeds, which could be dangerous to our health. Fortunately the only bananas we encountered were the same kind found in the States.

The government's literature also provided guidelines for tipping cabbies. Tipping was not customary and cabbies did not expect it, but if traffic was particularly heavy or they drove with extra care, we could show them our "appreciation."

Master Sergeant Ruddy followed me in the orientation briefing. He covered the salient points of the Southeast Asia Treaty Organization (SEATO), formed in 1954. SEATO came in the wake of the Geneva Accords, which had divided Vietnam at the seventeenth parallel and made the countries that once were French Indochina independent of France. He compared it to NATO for easier remembering, as a defense and economic pact. For us, the chief importance of SEATO was territorial; it affected, technically at least, where we happened to be. Thailand was a member nation. (In fact, SEATO as a whole did not join the United States in its military efforts less than a decade later in Vietnam, although some of its members did. It was a footnote to Southeast Asia history by 1977.)

Earl Kalani's responsibility was to report on King Rama IX, Bhumibol Adulyadej, also known as Phumiphon Aduldet. We would meet him, and the background was useful.

Born in Cambridge, Massachusetts, the king of Thailand had received his education in Bangkok and in Lausanne, Switzerland. In June of 1946, Adulyadej ascended the throne as king designate when his older brother, King Ananda Mahidol, was shot to death. However, the regents ruled the country until he was formally crowned Rama IX on 5 May 1950. Because Thailand was a constitutional monarchy, the crown carried no real power; and the king performed mostly ceremonial duties. However, we were advised that he did exercise considerable influence on the government.

The military staff briefed us extensively on the role of Gen. Thanom Kittikachorn, whom we would also come to know. Born in 1911 somewhere in northwest Thailand, he was educated at the military academy in Bangkok, joined the army, and rose through the ranks. Kittikachorn supported the takeover by Lt. Col. Phibun Songkhram in 1947 and, by 1951, had risen to the rank of major general. (He was a lieutenant general when we met him in 1956. Second in command of the army coup that brought

Gen. Sarit Thanaret to power, Kittikachorn would later succeed him as prime minister in December 1963 and served in that capacity until October 1973.)

### The King and I

King Rama IX was a man of many talents. An accomplished jazz musician and composer of popular music, he was a devoted fan of Woody Herman and some of the prominent black musicians of that time, including Wynonie Harris, Lloyd Price, Ruth Brown, Big Joe Turner, Louis Armstrong, and Duke Ellington, to name a few. I suppose he assumed that all black people knew and played jazz, because he sent a special messenger summoning me to talk about it!

The messenger seemed genuinely surprised to learn that I played no instrument of any kind, but the king was pleased enough just to talk about black music. I knew a lot about black musicians—enough to hold my own in conversation with him. We spent the majority of our time together discussing various musicians, one of whom was B. B. King.

When the king discovered that "the King of Blues" had spent some time in Lexington, Mississippi, my hometown, and that his family claimed mine as relatives, he wanted to know as much about him as possible.

He also seemed genuinely interested in learning more about the plight of minorities in the States, particularly blacks. We talked extensively about the difficulties that President Eisenhower was having with civil rights during those times. I shared with him my opinion on Eisenhower's apparent personal indifference to the black civil rights movement and his stance on using federal troops to desegregate the schools. In addition, I shared some of my personal thoughts on what it meant to be black in the armed forces and in the United States at that time.

The king also wanted my opinion of Secretary of State John Foster Dulles. He saw both Eisenhower and Dulles as aggressive anticommunists and advocates of the liberation of Soviet-dominated nations. We discussed Eisenhower's hopes to cut military expenditures. We also discussed his 1952 presidential campaign and his promise to end the Korean War.

Another important area of discussion was how the CIA covertly established anticommunist regimes in Iran in 1953 and Guatemala in 1954.

When my audience with the king was over, I went back to the base and wrote up my notes. I wasn't leaving that Green Beret experience to the risks of memory.

### The Mission: Cooperation and Conflict

Our mission in Thailand was a large and complex enterprise. We worked with three widely dispersed, isolated camps carved out of the jungles. One of our tasks was to teach the inhabitants how to prop areas up out of the Chao Phray River floods.

Our basic mission was to provide extensive Special Forces training for the Royal Thai Army, preparing and organizing a relatively large pool of highly qualified personnel to meet virtually any probability. For six months we would act as teachers of tactical shooting, guerrilla warfare, and jungle survival, including the latest concepts in administration, logic, communications, command-and-control, conflict (detecting disharmony in foreign governments), and training support.

The mission was a classic example of a successful operation run on a shoestring. The multiplier effect was also evident. We, a small number of dedicated professionals, indirectly produced thousands of effective counterinsurgency operators who could operate, whenever necessary, in their native environment. We planned to use tactics suitable to the surrounding terrain and to possible future enemy dispositions. Such an operation as ours did not require the huge logistical infrastructure that would eventually be erected in Thailand, as well as in Vietnam and Laos.

We were to conduct a wide variety of "paramilitary" operations sponsored by the Central Intelligence Agency, with whom we were closely associated at the time, although it was taboo to refer to the organization by that name. We knew it simply as "the agency." Even now, I find it difficult to say "CIA."

Our involvement with the agency became a story of both cooperation and conflict. Top CIA planners saw the threat on the ground and jumped at the opportunity to step into the role vacated by the French in 1954. They were seriously looking at the business of counterinsurgency—in other words, keeping a lid on groups that were trying to destabilize countries that had U.S. support. They also viewed Thailand's highland forests and jungles as potential bases and infiltration routes in event of open armed conflict to the east in Vietnam, Cambodia, and Laos.

It was important to the United States to help the Thais stabilize their diverse political, ethnic, and religious factions. World War II was less than ten years in the past, with much of its damage still unhealed.

Colonel Madding was perhaps the chief driving force during these early days in Thailand. A slender, soft-spoken, bespectacled man, he presented a quiet façade that concealed a dedicated, objective professional. He was one of the army's true experts, along with Captain Cramer and Sergeant Ruddy, on Southeast Asia and guerrilla warfare. Although he possessed a definite military bearing, his mild demeanor helped him to deal successfully with the Asians. In some ways, he reminded me of my father, a World War I veteran who also had an ability to see the big picture, wherever he was.

Like my father, Colonel Madding could cope, deftly, with whatever confronted him. General Kittikachorn, who served in Thailand's cabinet from 1947 until 1957, approved any reasonable request that he made. Under Colonel Madding's leadership, the 14th provided all of the early counterinsurgency and much of the conventional combat training, with the exception of a few small projects handled by the CIA.

Because of Colonel Madding's former connections and ongoing communication with the CIA, we knew we could depend on it for support of various kinds. One kind of support was its Air America planes and helicopters, which helped us move men and supplies to otherwise inaccessible areas. Flown by Air America and Thai pilots, this private air force included 123s as well as E-1, E-2, C-46, and C-47 aircraft.

I had already become familiar with the CIA, in the Philippines in 1948. In Thailand, its operations continued to amaze me.

We reported directly to the Office of National Security. They informed us that we were responsible for gathering and evaluating intelligence in the area—"information vital to the security of the United States." The agency coordinated the work of other agencies in the area, including the National Security Agency and the Defense Intelligence Agency.

One aspect of CIA involvement that astonished us was the freedom that agents had in their operations. A case in point: We noted that their "embassy individual" would arrive by Air America with a satchel of baht (Thai currency) that we suspected totaled hundreds of thousands of dollars. To this day, all I know regarding what happened was that the messenger showed up about every two weeks or so and disappeared behind closed doors. We had no idea whatsoever what happened next.

However, we did have firsthand knowledge of the agency's strong influence in other countries, including Taiwan, Korea, and Vietnam. We also concluded that the agency subsidized some of the political leaders in these areas and recruited services from wherever possible—local businesses, educational institutions, radio stations, and news agencies.

Because of our connection with the CIA, other agencies did not interfere. For the six-month span of this Thailand mission, the twelve members of our original 14th Special Forces team were precisely where we wanted to be—pretty much on our own.

### Training Thai Soldiers: Making Some Changes

The trainees moved through a morning of physical training as I stood at the edge of the field. Some were bicycling. Some were on the ropes. Some were running around the track, chanting an American cadence in English. Some were doing push-ups.

A young Thai sergeant, caught cheating on the last lap, whimpered softly as he struggled to do one more push-up. Beside him crouched a member of our team, shaking a fist and yelling, "Keep on going! You can make it!" Then, in a softer tone, he continued, "You can feel sorry about it later!" Was this *encouragement*, from a Special Forces trainer? Fort Bragg seemed a million miles away!

The Thai trainees were well-qualified soldiers, top-notch senior NCOs, junior and mid-level officers, and soldiers from all branches of the Royal Thai Army. Most of them already had Ranger training under their belts. They were all airborne, or paratrooper, qualified and held high national security clearances. They were also sharp as tacks in many areas of conventional warfare and had some superficial knowledge of Special Forces. Thus, their prior knowledge and training made our task of teaching special warfare and its concepts much simpler.

A Special Forces trainer assumes awesome responsibilities. Regardless of the trainees' professional status, at Fort Bragg we, as trainers, told trainees when to sleep, when to eat, what to wear, and how to think. We marched them to activity areas, inspected their barracks, ordered them to chow, and distributed their mail. We gave them permission to see the doctor and ensured that their uniforms met Special Forces requirements. We were very much concerned about the state of the trainees' relationships with each other, about the order of their finances, and about their lives in general.

We had the ability to advance the better trainees and retain the poorer ones. We recommended soldiers for recognition, at least in the sense of giving them more responsibility and support for a training mission, or for dismissal from the training cycle.

Stateside, we had the "capability," so to speak, to make their lives easy or to make them a living hell. "Break the troops down to a stick and build them back up into a tree," was the trainer's traditional philosophy.

One did not challenge or question the trainer at Fort Bragg. I vividly remember shouts during training cycles in the latter part of 1952 or 1953. Trainees did push-ups until the trainers got tired of watching. There were always some curses (no punches, though, and no broken arms). There were people puking all over the place. In those days, we surmised that the chain of command somewhat directed, if not forthrightly endorsed, such trainer authority and behavior.

However, the U.S. Army and the Special Forces recognized the immense potential for abuse in the training system. Our method of being "rough and prepared but fair" had been under serious discussion for some time. Consequently, a change began to take place throughout the Special Forces about the meaning of power, particularly in situations involving international troops.

Colonel Madding recognized some of the deep systemic flaws regarding power, and he set out to correct them. He and I, as his special advisor, discussed the matter in detail and agreed on modifications. Consequently, with the concurrence of the rest of the team, Colonel Madding implemented a new training philosophy for the 14th Operational Detachment. While our training objectives remained the same, we recognized that we were in Thailand as friends, in order to teach the trainees ways to survive and win. It did not make sense to push them around. We could not be the "abusive beast" with the Thai trainees if we expected them to respect us and learn from us. We had to respect them, and learn from them.

Although General Thanaret granted us complete leeway in making the training as rough as possible, Colonel Madding insisted that there be no heavy cursing, no humiliation, no house of pain. The days of the tyrannical Special Forces trainer were over—at least in our relationships with the international community.

Often, treating the Thai trainees respectfully—as Colonel Madding put it so well, "the way that you, as professionals, would want to be treated"—meant walking a thin line, somewhat like training them to "do as I say, not as I do." He always assured us that whatever discipline we dished out was soundly within the context of training "the best of the best." Of course, as force multipliers and trainers of future trainers, we had to impress upon them that they could not be too easy on *their* trainees. At the same time, we had to treat them, as trainees, with respect so that they would want to remain in the Thai Special Forces and would retain their esprit de corps and enthusiasm. Colonel Madding insisted that the best way to accomplish this was to tell these troops why. We had to tell them *why* the training would be difficult and *why* the training might be painful.

### The First Day: Information, Formation, and Fury

As a team, the 14th brought a wealth of experience into the organization of the Thai indigenous forces. We were in good physical condition, we were experts in all the Special Forces skills, and we collectively, at least, possessed the requisite language skills. Two team members spoke Thai. I spoke a little French and was fluent enough in Thai to carry on a decent conversation.

As one of the senior team members, I was in charge on the first day of training. At 0500 hours, the Thai troops scurried from their barracks. Even at this early hour, the morning's heat was withering and unforgiving, but not nearly as unforgiving as we would eventually be.

"Attention!"

The Thais scrambled into formation.

Although I must give them credit for having "snap," I was furious! One of the officers wore sunglasses, which was totally unacceptable. However, remembering Colonel Madding's mandate to proceed slowly, I did not say anything immediately.

I am a self-declared "nice person." I am not, however, a nice trainer in the sense of being too easy. Fair? Yes. Easy? Absolutely not! The primary objective of this first general briefing was to get to know the trainees. However, I wasted no time in addressing the importance of proper appearance at formation. My message to the troops—language barriers aside—went something like this:

"Over the next five to six months, you're going to become Special Forces trained personnel, some of the greatest cadres in the world. We will train you to infiltrate enemy-controlled territory and to contact and organize local dissidents for guerrilla operations. We will train you hard, but we will treat you fairly—across the board, regardless of rank.

"When you become trainers, you will have to search throughout the Thai army to recruit potential Special Forces trainees. Once you find them, you will work them hard. But you must not abuse them."

"We always want to convey the impression that we are civilized," I explained. "All people—we, you, and I—are civilized people, even though we are called upon to do hard things from time to time. When I ask others and you ask others to kill, you will expect them to do that.

"Nevertheless, when we tell them to stop, when you tell them to stop, we expect them to stop. We are still civilized and we must all follow the rules of good order and discipline.

"This is a tough thing to instill in people. However, it has to start right now in basic Special Forces training. It has to start with us as Special Forces trainers. There is no simple, perfect way to accomplish this. Colonel Madding's directives and my admonishments to you—are only theory. But in the reality of initial Special Forces training, you may be encouraging your trainees one moment and bawling them out the next."

I continued.

"We will learn together. We will teach you, and you will teach us. An essential aspect of learning is order. Special Forces groups must be orderly. Order is necessary regardless of rank. Order means confinement of individual needs and desires which, in turn, fosters teamwork, unity, and fighting machine dominance. As Special Forces troops, you will possess strong esprit de corps and intensive cross training. As a precaution against loss or injury to members of your team, you will know all phases of all specialties within the team. However, before we can get to that, simply lining up straight in formation is the beginning. We expect your formation to have the precision of a chessboard. And we expect your uniforms to be flawless."

I had already observed that a few of the senior-level officers were overweight. Some were spoiled. A couple were even slackers. I knew that such people tend to be losers; they probably would have difficulty completing training.

I went on, "There will be rigorous physical conditioning. A Special Forces operator must never be viewed in a negative light, as a slouch, a moron, or a crybaby."

Later that morning, I sent them all back into quarters to change into their U.S. Army–issued uniforms of athletic shorts and tennis shoes. Then, we went on a pre-dawn run. Even that morning I pushed them to run harder and faster. Although most of them were in good shape, shortly all were huffing and puffing. Because they spoke English, I taught them an American cadence to help them get through it: "Shut up! Take it!"

I continuously corrected broken strides, calling to the trainees who slowed and broke the beautiful clip-clop sound of shoes hitting the ground in unison. During the break, I quietly shared my overall assessment with them. "You know, it is unbelievable the shape you will be in later compared to where you are now."

During later phases of training, we sometimes had to institute disciplinary action. We could not slap or punch the trainees. We could not call them names. We could not deny them meals or water as punishment. We could not make them roll in the mud or assume the infamous "roach" position (in which we lay on our backs and shook our legs and arms like a dying cockroach, on occasion, at Fort Benning, Georgia). However, we could insist that they run around the trainee group and do push-ups, and we could use strong words. I had to reach deep within myself to find words that would express my anger—that is, words that would express my disgust and rage but were not too severe. I needed softer words that still motivated the group to be their very best. Given my training at Fort Benning and Fort Bragg, it was difficult for me to find such words and not curse.

But my former repertoire did change and came to include such phrases as "Dog-gone it, we just have to do better!" "I'm certain you're not block-heads." "Have you lost your minds today? We know you don't mean to slack off like this if you intend to be full-fledged Special Forces operators." "Boy, we're going to get pretty upset with all of you if you don't straighten out here because we want you to be the best." And so on, civilized indeed.

It was not easy to change our philosophy as trainers to accommodate the in-country task. The 14th demanded more of us as individuals than ever before. We were model soldiers, parents (even for the older Thai trainees), psychologists, and sociologists.

When the word spread that we were using a slightly different philosophy from the trainers at Fort Bragg, former comrades back in the States wanted to know if it was tough to make the change. Frequently, changing is tough because it is difficult to unlearn behavior. On the other hand, I came to internalize Colonel Madding's belief that a Special Forces trainer can be effective without being abusive or disruptive.

### Rifles, Rucksacks, and Parachutes

Thailand required specialized equipment and a considerable quantity of supplies to carry out both the training and day-to-day garrison activities. Available to us were special army-allocated "Table of Allowance" (TOA) and other organizational and individual equipment and supplies.

There was little, if any, special development or special acquisition of equipment for the Thai Special Forces trainees. Clothing and equipment, in most respects, were identical to what was available in all airborne units.

The M-1 rifle with mountain rucksack was always a part of our standard equipment. Individual equipment included the load carrying (rucksack) and other items used to support us in the field or on training missions. The equipment was generally referred to as TA-50 gear, because it was found in the TA-50 Series of the TOE. However, some equipment, like the AN/GRC-9 (nicknamed "Angry 9") radio, was somewhat new to us, although we had used them with the 77th and 10th.

We stressed how important it was for the Special Forces soldier to maintain his gear properly. We also made it known that gear was a soldier's personal support in the field, in training, and in combat.

As far as I can determine, we were the first troops to use the rucksack (nicknamed "the mountain") in Southeast Asia. The CIA made them available for the Thai soldiers and through our special requisitions from the States.

We emphasized that the rucksack is one of the essential pieces of equipment available to the Special Forces soldier. In it, we carried our clothing, our rations, and our sleeping gear. Unlike the conventional soldier's direct connection to supplies and the transportation system, the Special Forces soldier had to be prepared to survive for extended periods with only the items that he carried on his back. Any particular anticipated mission would dictate the extent of the load that a soldier would carry in his rucksack.

The rucksack is an exceptionally rugged construction. In our presentation, we described it as having a large cargo compartment, three external pockets, and a zippered map packet on the closing flap, all of which closed by buckles. It also consisted of an external tubular frame, a bellyband, and a weapons attachment strap, the latter two used primarily in mountaineering. (Although we did not do much mountain training in Thailand, we did teach quite a bit of the art. There are several points of attachment—for canteens, a bayonet, a regular entrenching tool, or other equipment. An H-harness holds a lowering line for rigging and jumping.)

Ironically, in this respect, one of the major strengths of the rucksack was also its greatest weakness. That is, its capacity for carrying so much equipment encouraged overloading. The cargo compartment could hold the issue down sleeping bag and cover and an air mattress. It could also hold extra uniforms and boots and still allow sufficient room for a number of C-rations.

The Thai soldiers learned the expediency of improvising to transform the mountain rucksack into the jungle rucksack by removing the unneeded straps and positioning it high on their backs, when necessary. They could add additional shoulder pads to help support the weight.

Although already effective parachutists, the trainees were required to become familiar with the T-7, the parachute we used for training. Primarily an escape device, we also used it as a means of parachuting into a specific combat or operations area. Thai airborne units still used T-5's of World War II vintage. (I believe we were the first to wear football helmets during parachute jumps in that part of the world.)

We had to teach the T-7's dimensions and workings (we also demonstrated the T-10) without written directions. Approximately 24 feet (7.3 meters) in diameter across the top, it had about twenty-three to twenty-seven pounds of gores made of nylon silk. In the top of that, in a slightly parabolic canopy, was a small vent hole in the center held closed by elastic bands. When we exited the aircraft and the canopy opened, these bands expanded to lessen the initial shock of deceleration. The bands, sewed into the so-called shock lines between the panels, passed through the top of the canopy. A harness of strong webbing passed over the wearer's shoulders, around the body, and between the legs.

With the aid of rubber bands and metal springs, the pack flew open when the metal closing line, called the ripcord, was pulled. With the ripcord attached to the aircraft, our weight pulled the canopy out. If we were free falling, pulling the ripcord caused a smaller parachute to eject from the pack that pulled out the main parachute. (When we were not using the parachute, our riggers folded it compactly and placed it into a container on our backs. Each team member could pack parachutes for jumping when necessary.)

### Training: A Multifaceted Approach

Field Manual 21-15 set the basic direction for all national training missions in Thailand. We had to be thoroughly familiar with it; in fact, we knew it almost verbatim, completely internalized it. The manual contained the standard operating procedures for various unit contingencies and provided details on the care and use of equipment.

Our aim was to replicate all training that we received at Fort Bragg and Fort Benning. As such, training covered a broad spectrum of areas. Special Forces history was one such area.

While the trainees' knowledge of the Special Forces concept was sketchy at best, they seemed enthusiastic to learn more about it. We filled them in on the details about how the Special Forces was modeled on various foreign commando-type units of recent decades and our forerunners in American history—actually some rather recent history. Another significant training area was the development of organization. We wanted to instill in the commanders the importance of the guerrilla battalion. In doing so, the first step we took was to build cadre and troop training programs, followed by specialized training in intelligence, sabotage, and subversion techniques. (Captain Cramer, our operations officer, Master Sergeant Ruddy, our detachment sergeant, and I were closely associated with cadre development for the 10th and the 77th.)

However, because we were to be in Thailand for only six months, we concentrated on weapons training. Although the Thais had a number of weapons ranges, we improvised our own (as part of training efforts), hiding them deep in the Lopburi forest. We taught the operation, maintenance, and employment of weapons common to a particular area. That is, the trainees became familiar with foreign weapons, and they, in turn, taught us about the weapons with which they were most familiar, particularly the weapons of their neighboring countries. A section of the training, labeled Target Interdiction Course, gave selected troopers training they would need to deliver precise rifle fire from concealed positions. It included marksmanship, watching techniques, covering, and camouflage.

"Do it right!" I howled at a line of Thai trainees lying face down in the dirt in front of me. With sweat dripping from my face, I could hear the ping-ping-ping of rifle fire off in the distance. As a senior instructor, I was teaching them how to retrieve Claymore mines, one of the most difficult tasks any soldier, including the Special Forces soldier, would ever face in actual combat or in basic training.

Removing a Claymore antipersonnel mine required a checklist and steady nerves. A Claymore is about the size of a hardback novel and uses a charge of C3 to scatter several hundred steel pellets. I remember the sequence (some things you never forget):

Check the inventory;
Get down in the prone;
Test the firing device;
Test the wire; and
Tie the wire.

The tasks had to be exact and in exactly that sequence. To get them motivated to learn this maneuver, some incentive was in order, so I appealed to their sense of competition. "Now all of us are going to go down to the range and we're going to be stars.

"What are you going to do?" I bellowed.

"Be a star. Be a star," the trainees responded weakly, in unison.

They then filed out into the field, to unreel the wire while sidestepping to keep from tripping. All moved carefully and methodically. All, that is, except a colonel who figured out that it is much easier to do this by walking backwards rather than sidestepping.

"You never turn your back on the enemy!" I admonished him. "I know you've taught this lesson to your troops. You do not want your Special Forces troops to forget it, either. Never, ever turn your back on the enemy!"

The reconnaissance course covered another key training area. Although we did not have time to go into detail, we did teach the technical procedures for special reconnaissance missions. We covered, at least on an introductory level, the topics of communication, concealment, intelligence collection, medical emergency, and day and night reconnaissance operations. We ended the section with a daylong field training exercise.

We put quite a bit of emphasis on the areas of operation and intelligence, using as a reference the Special Forces Operations and Intelligence Briefing, which qualified successful candidates for assignments as Special Forces detachment intelligence NCOs. However, contrary to the training at Fort Bragg, where the Operations Intelligence Course was strictly for intelligence NCOs, we did not make a distinction between noncommissioned officers and intelligence officers.

As intelligence trainees, the Thais learned to employ specialized intelligence techniques required by Special Forces roles and missions. They engaged in search and rescue, escape, and evasion activities. We taught them how to use general aviation support wherever they were operating. In addition, we educated them in effective air control and close air support.

The extensive training we provided on psychological operations was intended to show them how to demoralize the enemy by causing dissension and unrest among his ranks. At the same time, our trainees had to know how to persuade the local population to support the Thai or American troops. Each unit had its own intelligence audiovisual specialist, and the units accomplished their mission primarily by disseminating propaganda messages in the form of leaflets, posters, audiotapes, and broadcasts. We assisted the Thai Army in erecting a powerful communication system capable of reaching unconventional warfare teams anywhere in Southeast Asia. We anticipated that it would reach into China.

We taught the trainees hand-to-hand combat, an area of specialization for some members of our team and one in which I was somewhat of an expert. Although we did not place a heavy concentration on it, we let them know that hand-to-hand combat and night fighting were important aspects of the training they would receive during our time there. I did emphasize the extramilitary concerns of medical training and its importance to communities and to the teams themselves in any combat situation.

A couple of us gave instruction in military free falling (HALO). Several jumps required oxygen equipment. (We also invited the trainees later to hone their ability to pinpoint their jumping accuracy at base camp.)

We taught a limited course in "underwater operations training," commonly known as scuba diving. The course included the use of open- and closed-circuit scuba equipment and such techniques as long-range underwater swimming, which was not my forte or interest. Instead, I was heavily involved in the medical and physical aspects of the course.

We taught the theory of jungle survival, in spite of the fact that we more or less expected the Thais to train *us* in this area. For us, survival in the jungle was a course of study. However, for them, it was a way of life.

We included a section on civil affairs. This training mainly taught the units how to prevent civil interference with tactical operations, how to assist commanders in discharging their responsibilities toward the civilian population, and how to develop liaison with civilian government agencies.

### The "Best Qualified" Selection Process

The caliber of a Special Forces soldier is only as good as the criteria used to select the trainee. Consequently, we had to define which officers and senior NCOs among our Thai trainees were qualified to become Special Forces troopers. Colonel Madding and I undertook a personal mission to institute a procedure that the United States Army could use to select potential candidates for future Special Forces training anywhere in the world. He gave me direct responsibility for the effort.

In the "best qualified" evaluation system that I designed, each trainee had to qualify professionally and physically, demonstrating that he was capable of performing the duties expected of a Special Forces operator and of becoming an integral part of a multiplier team.

Each trainer kept a file, referred to as an Individual Selection Portfolio, of comments on each trainee throughout the six-month training period. The file included each trainee's assessment at both the beginning and conclusion of the training cycle, as well as the write-ups of ongoing interviews.

We noted their motivation, intelligence, independent judgment, demonstrated skills, and physical fitness. In essence, we evaluated their readiness for organization into light military units capable of conducting missions in times of war or peace.

Specific areas included an assessment of the trainees' ability to operate covertly as a team in conducting raids, demolition, infiltration, and psychological warfare. They would need such capabilities when the time came for them to train others in guerrilla warfare, internal security, and counterterrorism. They were also reviewed for their knowledge of techniques of rescuing hostages and protecting important personnel and critical facilities. Each member of the training team had access to the portfolios of all candidates and reviewed all entries in them before submitting them to the selection board for evaluation.

The board used a six-point cumulative checklist. Each point, 1 to 6, had plusses and minuses.

6+ Absolute Yes; top few; definite select.

5+ Yes; high in the pack; high in the group; clearly ahead of contemporaries and definitely must be selected to qualify.

4+ Solid performer; qualified and very responsible; fully deserves selection and should be selected.

3+ Shows potential; somewhat inexperienced; will do better after some additional experience; select with hesitation

2+ No; cannot make it because of the physical strain; not qualified; needs experience; needs additional physical training; must not be selected.

1+ No (Trainer must show cause why the trainee was not selected.)

To maintain anonymity, each member of the board had a number and voted as that number. We used a paper-and-pen scoring system. I verified and tabulated all results. After we had voted on portfolios, we ranked the candidates and determined the qualification cutoff line, which proceeded from the "fully qualified" to the "not qualified."

The portfolio evaluation approach was a definite asset in our mission. It exerted a tangible, observable influence on the administration of the Thai

Special Forces by providing a more formal system of record keeping. We learned later that the portfolios eventually extended to the selection board for officers and their promotions. The Thai armed forces accepted it in its entirety.

We recommended that other field training units adopt the approach, also. Indeed, it ultimately became useful to future trainers, which they conformed to the in-country situation.

### Graduation: Pomp and Circumstance

On 15 December 1956, most of the Thai trainees graduated—some with honors. We were proud to have worked with them. During the ceremony, I received an inscribed cigarette case and a special award from Gen. Thanom Kittikachorn. The oversized plaque reads: *In special appreciation to Sfc Chalmers Archer, Jr., for services rendered to Ranger Battalion Royal Thai Army, as advisor to Ranger Battalion.* Both the case and plaque are signed "General Thanom Kittikachorn, CG 1st Army" and dated 15 December 1956. The cigarette case is still in my possession. Both items show the three-headed elephant symbol of Thai nationalism, Thai parachute wings, and an inflated parachute.

The Thai soldiers' newly acquired Special Forces training, coupled with their existing background in airborne, ranger, and officer and NCO training, now qualified them to conduct Special Forces–related and other projects in Thailand and neighboring countries. In addition, they could teach deep penetration of enemy organizations, conduct reconnaissance missions, and identify target designations of weapons. However, we warned them that, just as the highly qualified and aggressive airborne and Ranger forces of World War II faced constant misuse, there would always be the pervasive temptation to throw Special Forces–trained personnel "into the breach."

Finally we again cautioned the new Special Forces troops to consider the consequences before becoming too rough on their trainees. We reminded them that as trainers they should not terrorize but, rather, from the first day, act as professionals, welcoming the new trainees as future members to the Special Forces ranks.

Because it is essential for teams to operate independently in the guerrilla organization, we reminded them, they would need to strive diligently to instill in their charges a sense of values, particularly regarding the importance of working together as a team and the necessity of playing by the rules.

As the speaker, a Thai officer, said (in English) at the close of the graduation ceremony:

> We all must work together to make this a better world. We must stand up and meet the challenges of the future Special Forces in Thailand, the United States, and elsewhere and we must train harder than ever before. We have to. As conflict continues to threaten dozens of our allies, the world will look more and more to the unique contributions and experiences of the Special Forces. The world will look to Special Forces troops, such as yourselves, who are carefully selected and who have trained so long and hard for Special Forces qualifications and the dangerous tasks like escape missions, maritime operations, and free-fall parachuting.

Indeed, the effectiveness of Colonel Madding's new philosophy for training foreign nationals had been tested and proven an overwhelming success in Thailand. Current and future Special Forces troops adopted it. In Thailand we refined our selection process and, in our reports to headquarters, we indicated the importance of doing a better job of finding Special Forces candidates. This applied to all trainees, American or foreign nationals.

### Out of Thailand

The 14th Special Forces Operational Detachment (Abn) (Area) was indispensable in the development of Thai unconventional warfare capability. We went into Thailand as a "special action" force to help build the country's counterinsurgency capability and its ability to train other units capability. We accomplished our mission, thereby giving the Thai program new breadth and depth.

We completed our tasks with singular devotion while living at times in remote villages and in presumed guerrilla-plagued northeast Thailand. Our presence in Thailand was known to few people, at home or in-country. The job we did would have been strenuous and dangerous under almost any conditions. Achieving the desired results in the training was often a slow and frustrating process. And there were real enemies among those who did know we were there; hostilities ranged from local interference to attempted assassinations of villagers who worked with us. However, we took it all in stride. For the Special Forces troopers, it was a part of everyday life.

We departed Lopburi, Thailand, on 16 December 1956 and left Bangkok the next day. Our destination: Okinawa, by way of Hawaii, as a cadre of the 1st Special Forces Group.

Members of the State Department's Special Medical Team to the Philippines, 1948. The vehicle and building were used as living quarters, dispensary, and community headquarters. Author is second from the right.

Sgt. Chalmers Archer Jr. as U.S. Army Air Force member, Philippines Health Team in 1949.

The author outside of barracks, Chanute Air Force Base, Rantoul, Illinois, 1950.

The 14th Special Forces Operational Detachment, Hawaii (circa 1956). Courtesy of Sgt. Maj. Robert Bennett (Ret.)

14th Special Forces Operational Detachment, January 1957, Hawaii. Six of the NCOs in this unit accompanied Capt. Harry G. Cramer Jr. (*rear row, fifth from left*) with "Team 3A" to Vietnam in June 1957.

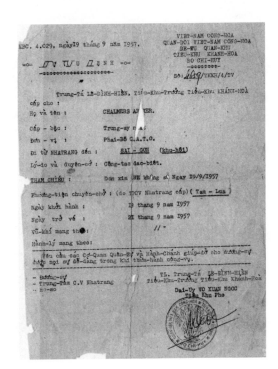

Author's Remembrance Award from Nha Trang, Vietnam.

Early photo of the 1st Special Forces Group (Airborne). Lt. Col. Albert Scott Madding, commanding, 1958.

Lt. Col. Albert Scott Madding, Commanding Officer, 14th and 1st Special Forces.

Change of command ceremony, 1st Special Forces Group, Airborne, 1958. Col. Marshall B. Wallack (*left*) and Lt. Col. Albert Scott Madding use a reserved parachute instead of a flag.

Author demonstrates aircraft exit during airborne training program.

Author at the Field Command Post, Laos, 1959.

The author at Cambridge University in 1986.

Madding Hall, Fort Lewis, Washington.

Col. John D. Balir IV, CO, 1st Special Forces Group (Airborne), Brian Zyglocke (age 10), and Maj. Harry G. Cramer III attending the dedication of Madding Hall, 9 February 1988.

Author at a book signing session for *Growing Up Black in Rural Mississippi.*

To prepare us for our stay in Taiwan, the government supplied us with background information about the country's culture and its position in the history of the Far East. Formerly called Formosa by the Portuguese, it fell to Spanish control in the seventeenth century, then to Japan in 1895. It had been nominally Chinese for little over a decade (since 1945) by the time we arrived. Needless to say, these transfers of power had not all been peacefully achieved.

As we soon discovered for ourselves, Taiwan's climate is subtropical and subject to monsoons, with seasonal wind changes. While winters are cold and dry, the summers are hot and rainy. Sometimes we could hardly see our hands in front of our eyes because of the heavy rainfall that occurred very often in the highlands. Typhoons occur at least annually and sometimes as often as three or four times a year.

Mountains appeared to be everywhere, covering the greater portion of the island. Yushan, which we called Jade Mountain, its highest peak, reaches more than thirteen thousand feet above sea level. In the mountains in the center of the country, everything stays damp because of the low clouds. This was the first time I had experienced an elevation where the clouds were lower than we were. They were so dense that you felt that you could wash your hands in them.

The scenic splendor and beauty along the mountain paths demonstrated every geographic feature that you could imagine. There are great changes in elevation in Taiwan, and that alone accounts for wide variation of vegetation. Moreover, the fruits and vegetables tasted better than any in Hawaii or elsewhere.

Water is everywhere in Taiwan. In this rugged country, villagers used bamboo to change the course of streams to water their crops. Freshwater springs flow beside the roads. Rivers, which originate in the mountains to the east, are generally short and beautiful, but not navigable. There are few good harbors on the eastern side of Taiwan.

The beautiful, richly productive western coast is home to most of the population. We were prepared by the government literature to find all kinds of ethnic groups living there, although it was a considerable time before we actually met any of them. We never knew exactly what tribes the people represented. Many of the ones with whom we came in contact were probably of Malaysian origin, according to my notes. We could sometimes tell their ethnic origins by their speech and dress and other ways of doing things, but we weren't there long enough to become experts in distinguishing one ethnic group from another with any certainty. However, we did know that the Chinese were only 17 percent of the population, and most of them had fled mainland China with Chiang Kai-shek around 1949. Although our research indicated that there was strife among the different ethnic groups, they appeared to get along just fine.

We arrived by aircraft, bivouacked overnight, and then boarded trucks to take us to the base at the eastern end of the island. We spent a couple of weeks going cross-country. There were roads on level ground, but we made most of the trip on footpaths—and sometimes on no paths at all. We had to rely on our compasses and on maps that were not too reliable. (Sometimes we saw signs showing the dates when American surveyors had posted them before World War II.) To find our way, we had to be skilled woodsmen. Here, I had no problem. Because I grew up on a farm, I could find my way around in the woods better than I could in cities.

We sometimes hired friendly villagers to help us carry our packs and equipment. They would often use oxen-drawn wagons or pushcarts. However, they could carry unimaginable loads on their backs and heads. Of course, we bartered a lot, but they were also happy to get "Taiwan dollars," as we called them.

Personally, I am innately curious, and I was excited about learning more about the peoples of Southeast Asia. Our orientation material made me hope that the trip to Taiwan would reveal understandings that we might otherwise have missed on the human side of things. I think all of us, in fact, came prepared to absorb the flavors of the country, and enjoyed doing so.

The Taiwanese that we met seemed to be very trusting and open. They readily shared information about their history and politics and about the country as a whole. In the cities, where Chinese culture prevailed, we saw very young children learning to write in Chinese characters, keeping the literary traditions alive on the island.

We "engaged the culture" extensively in Taiwan and met many uncommon people in the most remote and barely accessible places. We also encountered whole communities that had never been down to the main cities of Taipei or the other cities of Taiwan. They had lived in those mountains all of their lives. We were a pure curiosity to them—especially me, being black.

We operated out of Taiwan on numerous occasions. There were many training missions and exercises, at least two extended trips of six months TDY. As military training teams (MTTs), we rotated in and out, providing instruction in weapons use, tactical intelligence, planning, communications, logistics, maintenance, and more. Despite rumblings from fellow military people that Southeast Asians were not trainable, we knew better.

On one particular mission as the 14th Operational Detachment, we arrived in Taiwan on 14 June 1957. Colonel Madding served as commander; Lt. Col. Byrl D. Taylor as associate detachment commander. Our fundamental objective was to train the Republic of China cadre in all aspects of Special Forces operations and techniques. Fifty Chinese officers attended this training. Subsequently, these same officers established the first Republic of China Special Forces Training Center at Lung Tan, approximately sixty miles south of Taipei.

We also trained over a hundred selected officers and NCOs of Taiwan's guerrilla force in the basics of insurgency and counterinsurgency. The nucleus of the training included airborne qualification, Special Forces trade crafts, and scuba diving. Until this involvement, the United States never had an army group accomplish so much for another nation. Overall, we became involved in almost every aspect of the Taiwanese Army and trained several counterinsurgency battalions.

We served without fanfare, often with no identifying patches or insignia, operating mainly in civilian clothes. (However, we did often wear our berets.) Our low profile did not diminish our sense of the importance of our mission. We were convinced and preached that counteraction was the answer to communist expansion and subversion and the communists' so-called wars of liberation.

Our big picture for Taiwan was to reintroduce to—or reinforce in—the Taiwanese the attitudes and behavior that had won mainland China for Mao Tse-tung and were winning Indochina for Ho Chi Minh. We intended to influence the emotions, motives, and behaviors of the Taiwanese government from top to bottom beginning with Chiang Kai-shek. Our mandate included any organization, group, and individual. This objective in itself drew heavily upon our ability to work with foreign troops, specifically to work effectively with the Taiwanese in a variety of military exercises with an eye toward possible foreign conflict. It really tested our maturity and experience. It also immediately taxed a bit our military, language, and cultural skills.

We internalized and attempted to advance a limited form of Mao Tse-tung's theory of war. In essence, he believed that guerrilla units eventually evolve to a military phase, where they engage the enemy not in fixed battle but always on the move: mobile warfare. Mao said: "When the enemy advances, we retreat. When the enemy halts, we persist. When the enemy tires, we attack. When the enemy retreats, we pursue."

During those times, there were elaborate briefings. We set up a demonstration area. This began with the introduction of the members of the Special Forces A-team. Some of us spoke fluent Mandarin and explained our positions in both English and Chinese, but my Chinese wasn't quite that good. Most of us, in fact, had to memorize some of our speeches describing various aspects of weaponry, medical training, construction, and so on, to make the material easier to translate.

During this period, we augmented the Taiwanese Special Forces detachments by developing intelligence, military support, and medical departments right in the field. We were busy! We made concrete progress in all areas. My primary duty was as a medic; we set up temporary hospitals, helped build temporary schools, and dug latrines.

Some distance from Taipei at a small military installation, the 14th established and ran a parachute school. We actually constructed the training apparatus for the airborne course. We had access to the C-130 "Black-birds." (I believe that about the time of our second trip we also had access to a number of C-47 and C-46 aircraft.) My understanding is that we got the first shipment of the 130s assigned anywhere in the world.

We were accustomed to all the customary kinds of strange and unexpected obstacles, but the jump school actually started on time. In about a month, the school opened and a group of really uninspired Taiwanese showed up for the training. It was rough for both them and us. However, the mission was a complete success. (An enthusiastic Chiang Kai-shek was on hand for graduation and parachute jumps.)

We produced a detachment of Taiwanese airborne combat specialists who were also Special Forces specialists. They were ready at a moment's notice to infiltrate by air, land, or sea behind enemy lines; they could also establish and train large guerrilla forces to serve as multipliers.

All the time we had to make certain that our counterparts absorbed the fundamental characteristic of Special Forces flexibility. We approached the unconventional systematically but always with regard to human error and other unpredictables. In other words, we taught them to keep their cool regardless of the situation.

One thing we had to convey to our counterparts was that preparation for special combat is different from conventional preparation. In unconventional warfare, the individual soldier plays an important role in designing and getting ready for the mission. It is a team job.

We put the young troopers through the same training we had received on security terminology, patrolling, raids, and ambushes. The classroom was an open-air shelter with benches for the students and a small blackboard—it reminded me of the first school the black community built in Tchula, Mississippi. Each of us took turns explaining the basics. We would teach a lesson and then take them out for trials. At first, they would bunch up and make too much noise. They initially knew nothing about immediate action drills, but they soon learned. Then they were eager!

After many training sessions, we would call everyone together, usually for elaborate dinners prepared by the Generalissimo's staff. The Chinese believe in celebration with meals. Actually, these were often after-action reviews, miniportions of the instruction. We discussed what went well and what did not go so well. The Taiwanese viewed our presence as a morale booster. Our living, eating, and drinking in the field with them showed that we appreciated what they were going through.

One thing we stressed was that defense against armed subversion is not a popularity contest. All military, political, economic, intellectual, and sociological actions would focus upon eliminating the root causes of the trouble in a particular country. The rebels themselves had to be isolated and their arguments defeated. We also made it clear that in addition to direct counterguerrilla operations, environmental improvements and population and resource control are some of the greatest tactics in the world to maintain or restore internal order. During these critiques, we reminded trainees that their responsibility reached beyond their country's borders.

We trained Special Forces teams in Taiwan to carry out vital and strategic missions with or without the help of guerrilla units. In other words, they would "multiply." When it came down to a decision, they could serve as fighting units if necessary.

I can enthusiastically say that we of the 14th Operational Detachment in Taiwan were the cutting edge of United States foreign policy in that critical era. In Taiwan, as elsewhere, we set a standard for achieving objectives no matter how difficult the circumstances or how dangerous the adversary.

### Getting to Know the Generalissimo

We talked with General Chiang Kai-shek and his staff extensively on this particular mission in 1957. We were attempting to shape the attitudes, inclinations, and expectations of the Special Forces in Taiwan generally, toward a more "hearts and minds" approach. The Generalissimo always seemed very interested.

Our team had the opportunity to share extended dinner discussions with Chiang around this time, during our training on Taiwan. He seemed to take a particular liking to Colonel Madding and to me and other members of the 14th. He would invite us to elaborate dinners at his favorite cafes. In addition to exchanging pleasantries, we discussed the future of Special Forces for the world and for Taiwan.

These dinner discussions with Chiang Kai-shek during our visits to Taiwan, or the "New China," were opportunities to gather intelligence during our training missions. They were also opportunities to reassert the princi-

ples that drove Special Forces. As president of the country, he had to face
the fact that, despite U.S. support, he had lost to Mao Tse-tung. He became
convinced that special warfare was of the utmost importance. The support
of the common people, he had to agree, was paramount in pursuing any
kind of military objective.

By the time that Colonel Madding joined us, he was able to continue to
convert the Generalissimo to an enthusiastic proponent of Special Forces.
We encouraged his staff to do positive things for the people and continue
to gain friends for the government. His troops were not strong in this area,
reflecting shortcomings in his earlier tenure as a national leader.

Chiang was a shrewd, smart man. Although old at this time, his innate
intelligence was still quite evident. He now saw the battlefield as being in
the hearts and minds of the people, not as brute force. Ironically enough, a
decade later we would watch the United States try to wage a conventional
war in the same part of the world, with the same results that Chiang
suffered.

### International Implications

Meanwhile, we were kept informed of events in other parts of Southeast
Asia. The elections that Ho Chi Minh had expected to win in 1956 never
happened; he would have to take all of Vietnam some other way. South
Vietnam was riddled with factional strife, aggravated by the methods of.
Ngo Dinh Diem, the U.S.-supported president. A dedicated anticommunist, Diem was not, in fact, democratically inclined. His goal was not to
move his people to freedom and democracy. The events in Vietnam had serious implications for Chiang Kai-shek, as they did for Indonesia, Malaysia, and the Philippines.

In the field, we operated on assumptions and conclusions that were different from those of most people in Washington, D.C. (The secretary of
defense at that time was Thomas Gates and the secretary of state was
Christian Herter.) As the 14th Operational Detachment Forces, we could
see what was happening in Vietnam. In my opinion, one of the major mis-
takes that Washington made during these years of crisis in Indochina was
in not listening to field reports from Special Forces people. We were convinced that we should have been encouraged to render reports for consideration and to make more recommendations.

Our reports indicated that there should not be an increase, particularly not a massive increase, in the number of U.S. personnel in Southeast Asia. (I am not certain of the number of troopers we had in the 1st Special Forces, but it was actually the 14th Detachment and sister units that were operational units.)

Colonel Madding was firmly against our involvement in conventional fighting as opposed to teaching others to be teachers. However, it seemed that the concept of Special Forces block building was losing its acceptance to people in Washington.

What we tried to stress for all during the mission was that success in guerrilla warfare depended very much upon programs such as ours and that it was a viable option. We tried hard to make it known that military action alone would not defeat some aggressors unless there was some type of counteroperation from within. We were likewise determined to point out that information coming out of Taiwan from some sources appeared to be inadequate. Since we lived with the people, we knew what was going on and reports rendered were at first hand. The only thing we asked of the administration in Washington was that it analyze our reports, not make any snap judgments, and accept the reports with open minds.

One important reason we represented the United States in Taiwan was to help the people improve their general standard of living through better crop-raising and animal husbandry methods. However, another aim was for us to help the people live their own lives without outside interference.

Not far from our minds at any time was the possibility of training guerrilla forces from various other areas on a large scale in Taiwan. We would train them to become operators on the mainland and to train in other areas such as Laos, Cambodia, Indonesia, Korea, the Philippines, and other Asian countries. The Taiwanese would help and develop, train, support, and direct these forces.

In the overall context of concerns in Indochina, the training operation in Taiwan was relatively small in size and cost, but it had enormous potential for blunting the effect of communist insurgency throughout Southeast Asia.

The objective of the United States in the Taiwan Strait was to prevent conflict until the People's Republic of China (mainland) and the Republic of China on Taiwan settled their differences peacefully. We helped pass the word on that the United States would come to Taiwan's aid in case of an attack from the mainland.

Taiwan was just the place for anyone to fully recognize that any conflict was in the minds of the people. This would be President Kennedy's assessment a few years later, and the one that we wanted to press at that point. (Kennedy had utmost faith in the effectiveness of guerrilla warfare.)

We could confirm Chairman Mao's analogy of guerrilla warfare with fish swimming in a sea full of real or potential enemies. Popular support—the winning of hearts and minds—was indispensable. However, we found it difficult to sell this to some Chinese there in Taiwan, probably because Chiang Kai-shek had a somewhat different philosophy.

Many military leaders in the United States at that time still believed success in war was on the side of the big battalions and divisions. They did not see anything unique about the "wars of national liberation" and concluded that the conventional tactics and training were sufficient. Therefore, all our recommendations to them appeared to fall on deaf ears. This may have been because they believed in the philosophy of "get there the firstest with the mostest."

We submitted white papers concerning the situation in Taiwan, remembering that we were in a nonthreatening situation, different from the volatile climates of Laos and Vietnam. We wanted Washington to know that if events continued to proceed in the way they were going, disaster would follow. The situation in the whole of Indochina and Asia could worsen terribly. We warned that things were changing so rapidly that predictions could be unreliable but that, given the terrain of Asia, we should be prepared with many options. We emphasized that the solution had to be primarily political and economic.

Given that defined military objectives for Southeast Asia were not coming from the leadership in that part of the world, we recommended the expansion of covert operations throughout Asia.

## 5  <u>*VIETNAM, 1957*</u>

We were going to South Vietnam to train Special Forces for the Army of the Republic of Vietnam (ARVN). Colonel Madding had requested and received the authority, at least theoretically, to run the show on his own. The CIA agreed to provide support for this 1957 mission, mainly by placing its Air America planes at our disposal.

The Special Forces mission to Vietnam was similar to those conducted in many other parts of the world. This was before counterinsurgency became both a popular word and an assigned mission. Throughout Asia, mobile training teams (MTTs), of which we were a part, helped friendly nations develop their own Special Forces. Several other Special Forces teams were committed to roles such as ours in Vietnam.

In our briefing at Fort Bragg, we had learned that the United States' participation in Indochina, though quiet, was not small. As a silent partner of the French, the Americans provided nearly a billion dollars to the country before the fall of Dien Bien Phu in 1954. After the signing of the Geneva Accords that year, U.S. aid became direct and started its long trend upward. American advice and money went toward building a conventional army to repel a possible Korean-style invasion from the North. The U.S. mission fell in line with this idea.

The program overall was well conceived and well executed. The 14th Operational Detachment began to plan development and expansion of special units in South Vietnam's armed forces. We were to develop guerrilla warfare units tailored for behind-the-lines activities in conventional and counterinsurgency conflicts. Our long-range mission: to provide South Vietnamese area teams with the capability to train a regiment and other units.

Our immediate objective was to provide basic Special Forces training for eighty-two handpicked officers and enlisted men. A small number of dedicated professionals would produce thousands of effective counterinsurgency operators who in turn could operate in their native environment using tactics suitable to the terrain and to the enemy's disposition. We were to help build an entire national Vietnamese Special Forces. In addition, we were to lay the groundwork for a revolutionary development program. In later years, Vietnamese Ranger battalions proved among the best of the Republic of Vietnam (ARVN) infantry units.

Initially security was tight and secrecy essential. We were to function with little fanfare, wearing primarily civilian clothes with no identifying patches or other insignia. The clothing stipulation was nothing to take lightly. If we had been captured, the Geneva Convention would not have protected us. Execution on sight was likely. However, this deliberate low profile did not continue throughout our stay in Vietnam.

### Field Diplomats: Trainers as Envoys

The 14th Operational Detachment was well prepared to train troops and the foreign populace to deal with guerrilla forces and tactics and to defend themselves against enemy attacks. (Of course, we would work shoulder to shoulder with them if there were attacks.) However, there was another critical side to our mission: winning the goodwill of the South Vietnamese people. Teaching solely the importance of "kills" and "weapons counts" in our view was inadequate.

Of course, we knew that some military actions might produce short-term gains—which could also ultimately result in greater long-term losses. As Sergeant Ruddy told us (it's in my notes from his briefing): "We must always take into account political consequences of actions that could at the time appear purely military. We must always be assured that military actions do not cause the people to become our enemies or enemy sympathizers."

Colonel Madding constantly reminded us of the importance of earning and maintaining support for the military through carefully conceived, prepared, and executed nonmilitary as well as military actions. He expected us to stress the vital need for the highest level of performance and discipline in the field. Thus, we taught the importance of good troop deportment in politically sensitive areas. This included fair and considerate treatment of the local populace.

According to Colonel Madding: "All of us in this must realize that the official and 'of the mind' effects resulting from lack of concern for people could cancel even the most brilliant hot war victory." Consequently, we were ready and eager to help develop indigenous potential wherever we found it.

In performing our duties, we received two passports—one military and one civilian. The South Vietnamese government also granted us diplomatic immunity. Truly, we were "ambassadors" in every sense of the word.

### Training Vietnamese Teams

Our primary mission was to bring the Vietnamese Special Forces units up to the same level as our American basic unit, the twelve-man A Detachment, commonly known as the A-team. Later, we provided advanced training for the B and C teams and field headquarters for A-teams.

The indigenous teams' organizational structure mirrored our Special Forces command team as taught in the States. It consisted of two officers and ten enlisted men. The officers, a captain and a first lieutenant, served as the commanding officer and executive officer, respectively. Most of the enlisted men in the team were senior sergeants, with a master sergeant serving as team sergeant and an intelligence sergeant being the second-ranking soldier. The intelligence sergeant was responsible for supervision of the day-to-day operations of the team, including the recruitment and training of agents (there were no superenlisted grades at that point).

Our mandated Special Forces role at this point was twofold. First, we were to provide training on how to infiltrate enemy territory either by parachute or by sea (in boats or with underwater apparatus) and across land routes. Second, we were to provide training in all aspects of psychological warfare. The purpose was to fan the flames of anticommunist sentiment among civilian irregular troops and the citizens of the enemy country as well, so as to generate fear and mistrust of their government.

Captain Cramer, our operations officer, recommended to Colonel Madding that, along with the regular training of Special Forces teams, we help the Vietnamese develop special detachments. These units would include specialists in public health, education, sanitation, civil administration, public works, and forestry. He suggested that we also provide psychological operations training on radio and leaflet propaganda, public information, entertainment, and education. He likewise endorsed active psychological operations, although only to a limited extent.

We trained two of the Vietnamese team members to serve as medical specialists. While some instruction involved detection and treatment of local diseases, understandably most of the training was in the care and treatment of war wounds.

We trained two communications experts for each team. They improved local communications by learning the art of repairing, using, and maintaining radio equipment. We also trained two demolitions engineering specialists in everything from building small bridges to destroying them. They worked mainly on small civic action projects.

One light weapons specialist and one heavy weapons specialist completed the teams. They would instruct in their specialties and help develop agent networks.

Everyone on our team spoke at least one second language, and we encouraged the Vietnamese to learn at least one other language also, preferably of a neighboring country. Like their American counterparts, each Vietnamese team member was cross-trained in at least two basic team skills. For example, medics could construct an accurate mortar barrage to blow up the enemy's rail lines and bridges, as well as efficiently care for the sick and wounded. In addition, each team member became an expert in hand-to-hand combat. Benefiting from our ranger training, they learned how to protect themselves. We blended judo, karate, wrestling, and boxing techniques into a lethal brand of bare-handed, close-up fighting. (They also became expert parachutists.)

The Vietnamese welcomed us as concerned professionals who helped their local communities. (I gave them some suggestions about farming methods, too.) Relations among our team, the military, and the people were mostly cordial. Some of their officers trained at West Point, at the Command and General Staff College at Leavenworth, and in other service academies in the United States. Others were educated and trained in North Vietnam.

We performed our diverse and unglamorous jobs well; Vietnamese teams that we trained were later able to join counterguerrilla forces in the country to harass and raid Viet Cong supply routes and base areas along the Ho Chi Minh Trail, if it came to that. Eventually, they acquired the capability to erect powerful communication networks capable of reaching unconventional warfare teams anywhere in the region.

### Making Something out of Nothing

Because officially we were not supposed to be there, we also were not supposed to be supplied with food, shelter, or other necessities, to say nothing of conveniences. We had to live off the land. I often get questions such as, "But how did you survive? Where did you find tools? Where did you find food?"

Resourcefulness—a "can do" attitude—got us through much adversity, and many problems in actual combat and in just plain day-to-day survival. We knew that guerrillas were as vulnerable as soft-shelled crabs in a "great big world" and had to remain hidden in areas difficult for counterguerrilla forces to penetrate. We also knew that we had to teach them, and learn from them, how to survive from day to day in the rugged mountains, overgrown swamps, and dense jungles of the region.

In our jungle survival training in Panama (I also taught survival there and in other countries), we were taught to survive completely off the land, to build our own "hootches" (shacks) and our own smokehouses. Besides that, we even made our own bows and arrows. We carved hatchets and cutting-edge tools from rocks for skinning game. But my best survival training was my first: growing up in the Depression in the rural South. Often, in trying to deal with a Special Forces situation, vivid images of Papa trying doggedly to repair broken farm equipment rushed to the forefront of my mind.

"You can make something out of nothing, son," he would say looking up from his task. "All you got to do is have the will to find a way, and there is always a way." That's how I learned resourcefulness.

In Southeast Asia, the problem often was simply finding enough suitable food. We soon learned that practically everything was edible, including rats. It is necessary to boil rats until all flesh is off the bones (in case you ever need to know).

We often ate lots of monkey meat and water buffalo. We skinned the monkeys and hung them in the smokehouses. To me they looked a lot too much like human beings. Water buffalo was good for a variety of uses: the hooves for tea, the skin for warmth, and the intestines and all other parts for food. We built grills out of bamboo, propped them over the cooking fires, and let the meat smoke for extended periods. This process produced a large amount of cured jerky that lasted almost indefinitely without spoiling.

Ants, a delicacy in many Asian countries, are almost 100 percent protein and were a part of our diet. The large red ones (sometimes called "fire ants" in the States) are attracted to a particular type of sweet leaf. We would boil a pot of water, dip the leaves filled with ants in it, and make soup.

Away from camp we often lived directly off the forest. We consumed our share of chicken-fried python, Big Red Ant Soup, and monkey meat. Not nicknamed "snake eaters" for nothing, we ate snakes galore. However, we had to be extremely careful in handling the ones that we ate. Certain snakes were especially poisonous, being both hematoxic and neurotoxic. That is, their bite broke down blood and nerve cells. We were advised that if bitten by certain snakes on a small extremity (such as a finger) to take a machete and cut it off immediately—that is, not to wait until the toxin spread. Even if you cut off the extremity, some of the poison could get into the system; and you would need an injection of antivenin.

The one asset that we relied on was our wits, remembering that they were always with us. This philosophy carried over into military strategy and into unit tactics. Potential tactics—given the size, training, and morale of forces, the types and number of weapons available—usually limited strategy, we found. The terrain, weather, capability, and location of the enemy forces posed ambient factors.

Because appropriate tactics were dependent on strategic considerations, we frequently cast aside a standard tactic completely because it did not apply to the prevailing objective, offensive, defense, elements of surprise, security, or the unity of effort. Therefore, we had to use our imagination. Moreover, during those times when the ideas that came to mind seemed preposterous, I would find myself remembering Papa saying, "You can do it. Find a way or make one!"

### The Black Witch Doctor

The enemy resented our disruption of their plans for conquest. The rumor was that there would be attempts to eliminate us. Psychological warfare began to heat up around us. Certain elements tried to intimidate the villagers into resisting us by spreading propaganda through publications and other forms of media indicating that we were feeding them poisoned food. Their attacks on me were especially vicious, accusing me of being a witch doctor, a practitioner of "bad medicine." I believe they singled me out because they had heard something about witch doctors from African folklore.

The specter of the blatant racism that I endured in the Philippines again reared its ugly head when the communist guerrillas took advantage of my race in Vietnam. Although racism was terrible in other countries—Hawaii, Great Britain, and even my beloved United States—by far, none exceeded what I had experienced in the Philippines. The times were indeed cruel, but they did not break my pride or self-confidence.

Just as in the Philippines, "playing the race card" did not work in Vietnam either. Instead of viewing me as someone (or "something") to be feared or despised, many Vietnamese were eager to learn about me. I spoke to them knowledgeably about the true meaning of the services provided by a "witch doctor." Most importantly, I could relate to them about the burden of suffocating discrimination both within and outside of one's country, similar to what many of them had faced. (The population of Vietnam consists of many factions, many of which despise each other.) Subsequently, the Vietnamese singled me out in a highly positive way. Several of them stated that they grew to respect the Special Forces more because of the assistance that I gave them.

### Nha Trang: First Death in Vietnam

Early on 21 October 1957, we left town for the place, about an hour away, where we were to hold graduation exercises. It was still dark, a couple of hours after midnight. As Nha Trang's crowds retired to their homes, the people who frequented the local bars and cafes lingered. The burly street vendors attended to their business of dispensing the last bundles of flowers and boxes of rice cakes from their small sidewalk stalls. Everything seemed natural, a night scene no different from the ones we had witnessed many times before during our stay.

Nevertheless, for us, something was different. The morning before, troops had captured and detained two suspected North Vietnamese soldiers who, under interrogation by Captain Cramer, revealed what we had really known all along: There would be an attempt on our lives in the near future. Although we had felt vulnerable since Hawaii, this revelation hastened our first real feelings of "war." Little did we know that death would come calling before the day would end.

In some respects, the terrain of Vietnam was ominous, filled with mountains that towered thousands of feet above stream-laced valleys. These mountains, covered largely by jungle, rain forest, or elephant grass, limited our access to the main camp. There were certain obvious dangers in the geography of this backwater corner of the world, a place where anything could happen. This kind of terrain was home to insurgents and full of them. We, the increasingly recognized American Special Forces team, along with highly trained Vietnamese detachments of specialists, were tempting targets.

Nevertheless, for now it was business as usual. We had to prepare for the next day's scheduled graduation and demonstration by the Vietnamese troops. Only two roads led to the graduation and demonstration area. Because we did not know exactly what to prepare for, we felt like sitting ducks. Moreover, we were.

With this in mind, we set out in a well-fortified column, fully alert to the possibility that something serious might happen either en route or at the graduation area. The headquarters detachment maintained a central reserve; if anything were to happen, every man and vehicle not otherwise engaged would automatically become available for evacuation and support. We maintained extensive communications surveillance with an aerial patrol helicopter provided by the commanding general of the United States MAAG (Military Assistance and Advisory Group), Vietnam, in Saigon. With the reconnaissance team screening for movement, we felt relatively secure.

The column reached the site without incident after about an hour on the road. We proceeded to set up a number of defense weapons. As "field diplomats"—teachers, trainers, and leaders—we did not ordinarily include machine guns in our defenses. However, because of the nature of the location, we surmised that extra precautions were necessary.

Around three o'clock on the afternoon of 21 October, a helicopter spotted movement along the far edge of the graduation area. Reacting with a valor borne of discipline, Special Forces training, and desperation, we responded to the situation.

Although it seemed like an eternity, the artillery barrage lasted only about fifteen minutes—long enough to critically injure Captain Cramer. When the first mortar rounds hit, I assessed the situation. It took me a couple of minutes to reach him; he was not quite dead. With serious head wounds, he still attempted to sit up. With the help of two Vietnamese Special Forces people, I placed him in the back of a two-and-a-half-ton utility truck (what we called a "deuce and a half") for immediate evacuation to the general training area.

The exact sequence of events thereafter is still hazy. As clearly as I can recall, by this time SFC Lester J. Ruper walked up to me completely covered with blood. His badly mangled right arm hung loosely at his side, his hand blown off completely. I could see the white of the exposed bone. Although badly injured, he was coherent enough to speak.

"Archer," he muttered.

"Yeah, Ruper?" I replied.

"You remember that hand you used to shake? Well, I don't have it anymore," he muttered, before collapsing to the ground at my feet.

I knelt down and began to administer the then accepted treatment for severe limb wounds such as his. I placed a tourniquet around the fleshy part of the arm where his hand had been. The bleeding stopped immediately. (Standard treatment at the time, tourniquets are no longer favored in such cases.) Quickly, I reached down, placed my hands under his armpits and pulling, dragging, and cursing, I moved him the short distance to the truck where Captain Cramer, barely thirty years old, lay dying.

After checking again to make sure that Sergeant Ruper's tourniquet remained secure, I turned my attention back to Captain Cramer. He was unconscious, but his body still moved spastically, as if he were attempting to sit up. Although I knew that it would have taken a miracle for Captain Cramer to survive his wounds, I wanted to reassure myself that I was doing all I could to save his life. I unfastened the chinstrap of his helmet. From the nature of the flow of blood, I knew the main wound was probably under the right armpit. As I tried hard to bandage it, I sensed that my efforts were in vain. In a matter of seconds, he was dead. I could not speak; my lips were moving, but no sounds came out.

By this time, two Vietnamese Special Forces medics had come over to get help with the other injured and dying soldiers. I turned my attention to them. Jumping from the back of the truck where Captain Cramer's body lay, I sprinted twenty or so yards to an undamaged truck. What sounded like small-arms fire and mortars exploded in the background. Running through the helmet-high elephant grass, I reached the outside of the truck and stood on a small log with my back to the noise behind me.

The motor in the truck was running, and I spotted a Vietnamese soldier slumped over inside. For some reason, I tried to cut the motor before attempting to rouse him to life. He did not move. The guy was about five feet nine and had to weigh at least 160 pounds—a large man for an Asian. Leaning into the truck, I could see the blood spewing from a bullet hole in his neck. I snatched open the door and struggled to pick him up, but he would not budge. Apparently, his foot had caught on something.

Since I could not free the trapped soldier, I jumped down from the truck and ran back through the grass to another Vietnamese soldier. Although I was certain that he was dying, I grabbed him and pulled him to safety. One Vietnamese Special Forces soldier running near me took two bullets in the leg and went down.

Then, I turned and ran back to the truck to try again to free the trapped Vietnamese soldier. I just could not get him out. He died right in front of my eyes as Captain Cramer had done a few minutes earlier. Knowing he was dead, I left him to attend to the other injured soldiers. As I worked on them, I was stunned, yet amazingly calm. I suppose I was in some kind of a daze. Just the same, other casualties demanded my attention.

"I can't move. I can't feel anything," whispered a wounded Vietnamese lieutenant. After checking him over, I told him that it appeared his neck was broken or out of place.

About six other local NCOs and officers suffered gunshot wounds. One was seriously injured in the right side of his chest and the others in their legs and stomachs. After emergency treatment, I immediately sent two Vietnamese soldiers shot through the abdomen to the rear area in an available truck. There were numerous other routine injuries inflicted to practically every part of the soldiers' bodies. At least five of them died.

In the early hours of 22 October 1957, I boarded a plane provided by Gen. Samuel Williams, commanding general of the United States MAAG, Vietnam, and escorted Sergeant Ruper and Captain Cramer's body to the Philippines, where I remained for a couple of weeks.

The attack occurred on the last official training date for that particular phase. (I do not recall if we trained more after the incident.) However, the training was an unprecedented achievement on our part and on the part of the Vietnamese Special Forces troops.

They were now qualified guerrillas and counterguerrillas, highly skilled, mature, teachers first, and fighters of uncommon physical and mental caliber. In short, we helped them develop into effective A-teams, fundamental blocks for all Special Forces groups. Unfortunately, they did not get a chance to continue to grow in that respect. Like many Special Forces trained teams, many became ranger-type soldiers.

*The Army Times* reported that approximately 140 armed attacks and terrorist acts were committed in the last three months of 1957. The Nha Trang incident was one of them. To this day, I am not certain where the attackers came from. They arrived too suddenly for words. Like lightning, they were upon us, cropping up where we least expected them. I recall that the burst of 30-caliber fire had barely died down before a tremendous series of blasts rang out from the hills toward the west. Grenades exploded in rapid succession over what seemed to be a wide area. Then came the sharp rattle of small-arms fire. We assumed that some of our attackers could have been present or former members of the group that we had trained. If this were the case, to get to us using small arms would have been relatively easy. After all, we had trained them well. All we know is that they got close enough to storm us. We assumed that people from the village area joined them in the attack.

These people may have been living as part of the civilian community. Behind that façade, they probably provided food, shelter, transportation, refuge, information, financial support, manpower, and countless other services and resources to the enemy. That day, apparently, they also provided direct attack support. We always had slept, night on end, with one eye open, wondering which of "our troops" would turn a machine gun into the area or roll a grenade under our bunks. We knew we had quite a way to go in winning the hearts and minds of all of the people. We were also smart enough to assume that we had enemy troops right there among us.

Nha Trang was the first time I was to witness such violent human death. Officially, I saved Sergeant Ruper's life and unofficially saved the lives of seven Vietnamese Special Forces troopers. The scene, indelibly etched on me as a young sergeant, left a lasting impact on my life. Even now when I find myself wanting to gripe about something, I think of that day in the middle of a Vietnam jungle and say to myself, "Hell, this is nothing!" Nevertheless, sometimes at the Special Forces reunions and meetings, if I hear "Taps" played in memory of some dead military comrade, I tend to swallow hard and often find something in my eye.

### In Memory of Captain Cramer

According to the standard histories of the Vietnam conflict, the first two American casualties of the war occurred on 8 July 1959, when Viet Cong commandos infiltrated the Bien Hoa air base. The standard historians did not see Capt. Harry G. Cramer die in Vietnam on 21 October 1957. I did.

Nicknamed "Hairbreadth" because of his experiences in Korea, Harry Cramer loved being a member of the Special Forces. Everyone knew it was a way of life for him. This graduate of West Point, class of 1946, he was a brilliant officer. His ability to retain information was phenomenal! For example, he learned to speak French and could memorize lengthy passages from the Holy Bible in only a short time. I had met only one other person in my lifetime who possessed such a photographic memory.

Having worked closely with him, I came to know him quite well. As a unit, we served together in a number of countries from 1955 to 1957.

Kathy McDonald, from columnist Jack Anderson's office at the *Washington Post,* called me on 2 June 1983, while I was visiting home in Lexington, Mississippi. Anderson had assigned McDonald to delve into the controversy raised by Captain Cramer's son when he discovered that his father's name was not included on the Vietnam Veterans Memorial in Washington, D.C. On 11 November 1983, Captain Cramer's name joined those of the others killed in action in Vietnam on that long wall, but the complete story still had not been told.

According to the Department of Defense, Captain Cramer died in an accidental explosion while training Vietnamese soldiers. That is simply not accurate! I know; I was there. He died in my arms. Also, when I found a report of the 1957 incident in which he died, it said that only Captain Cramer and one Vietnamese lieutenant were killed, when in fact nine additional Vietnamese soldiers eventually died.

When the Vietnam Veterans Memorial Fund was initiated in 1979, I offered its administrators information about Captain Cramer, Sergeant Ruper, and the role played by the 14th Operational Detachment, Special Forces. They refused to accept it. In 1982 I made the offer again. Once more, they declined, with no reason given. I can only surmise that it was because of someone's refusal to acknowledge that we were in Vietnam so long before the war became "official." Secrecy may have been dictated by the Department of Defense.

Telling his story here is a small tribute to Captain Cramer, the first of many great American patriots killed in Vietnam. He deserves official recognition. The role played by the 14th Operational Detachment should also be made known—in that war that lasted for *eighteen* years, not thirteen, as many people think.

In retrospect, I still find unbelievable the inconsistency of U.S. policy and the disappointing and inappropriate decisions that virtually canceled out our dangerous work in Vietnam in the fifties. I sincerely believe that, if allowed to proceed as planned, our operations would have succeeded, without the huge logistical groundwork the United States erected for the Vietnam War. Nor would it have needed to sacrifice thousands of young American military people who did not know the first thing about jungle warfare.

If the United States had begun more carefully in Vietnam, developing a counterinsurgency potential with a single agency, the situation most likely would have improved. This was true whether the operative entity had been the CIA or Special Forces, in small teams. Needed also was more research, followed by careful preparation for unconventional warfare. With this approach, the Vietnam situation at that time might have been an entirely different story.

# 6  *OKINAWA, 1958*

The 1st Special Forces Group (Airborne) went to Okinawa to train for its next mission early in 1958. I had been there before, right after World War II. Déjà vu: scenes from another trip to the island danced before my eyes. On that first tour, traveling throughout the countryside over the villages' paths and roads with the 839th Engineering Aviation Battalion, I had constantly stared into the face of Death. The brittle bones of skeletons were scattered everywhere, sunlight frequently reflecting off their dog tags. Remnants of weapons lay in open view, the aftermath of bloody battles.

This time, however, on pleasant mornings in the dark green woodland, wet branches slapped against our once starched, pressed fatigues and freshly shined boots as we headed out for our briefings. Water rushed over the glossy rust-colored rocks in the creek bed nearby. Birds chirped noisily in the trees all around us. Training sites in Okinawa were almost always set up near a creek or other running water. They were sometimes in the middle of hunting preserves or dense forests. Although mosquitoes and other insects were troublesome, the island's warm waters, coupled with the gentle breeze, made it a water insect's heaven. It was pretty good for people, too.

### Mission Preparation

Regardless of my memories of Okinawa's past and my pleasure in its present, the future called for my attention. I was now an experienced operator, a member of the 1st Special Forces Group (Abn). The 14th had served this unit as cadre in late December 1957. As I anticipated the activities of the day, I thought about how much I enjoyed being a part of this organization, not yet the famous Green Berets but already rich in unique Green Beret experience. My team members knew that Special Forces was my passion, my life. They often referred to me as "Sergeant Special Forces."

For me, there was always hope for tomorrow and a love of life, an eternal light within us. No one begrudged our team its crème de la crème status within the elite Special Forces family, because we had earned it the hard way! Therefore, during this early morning hour, I wondered, "Can things get any better than this?" I was still quite young—about to turn thirty—and of course immortal. And today was my day to deliver a presentation on teamwork.

Each team member was cross-trained in a number of skill areas. For instance, besides serving as the team's medic, I specialized in interpersonal and cross-cultural relations. Part of my job was to encourage sensitivity to the concerns of local populations, on Okinawa and wherever our leaders would send us.

Since teamwork was one of my favorite topics in the military, I warmed to the task.

A group as tight as this one had many characteristics of a marriage, although many of our vows of loyalty and mutual support were unspoken. To fulfill each other's expectations in the field, we had to respect ourselves and each other. I told them something like, "We must continue to be the ones who walk in when everybody else deserts. Although we do not celebrate our closeness formally as we celebrate marriage and the births of children, it plays a major role in our development as team members. We know that the ingredients of team closeness are loyalty, trust, generosity, acceptance, and honesty. Yet we know, too, that team closeness could be the most neglected relationship in the life of our group."

After dealing with some of the divisive factors that could put us at risk in the field, I continued, "I trust two things, my instincts and my team members." We all knew that we would soon be tested again, somewhere in the world.

Presentations like mine helped to maintain esprit de corps even when our next assignment was a mystery. It helped to have a big picture of world affairs and our role in it. We had heard that our team would be embarking on a mission of international significance sometime during the early part of the year. Possible destination: Laos. If the rumors proved to be true, it would be our first assignment to that country. This was a special time for unconventional warriors, and a mission such as the prospective one involved much more than readily met the eye.

I took notes at Commander Madding's briefings. He was very firm about the seriousness of this mission, telling us to work hard and always to look at the big picture—the ultimate effect that our missions might have on the political climate of Special Forces, the U.S. Army, the U.S. government, and our regions of interest.

We expected to continue as multipliers at the international level, leading and instructing amateur warriors to defeat larger regular forces. However, our job was understood to involve political science as much as the science of war. Seasoned by our experience in Thailand, Taiwan, and Vietnam, we felt confident that we could meet the challenge. At the same time, we sensed that our commanders were under tremendous pressures to adapt Special Forces to changes in the world situation and in U.S. foreign policy. We were fighting for our lives in more ways than one.

Soon we learned that, indeed, our team's next assignment would be Laos. We assumed that the order came from Commander in Chief Pacific (CINCPAC), although missions could originate from several sources. Most of our orders came directly from the office of the secretary of defense. Previously, our teams were primarily under the direct authority of a CIA entity. From our briefings, we learned that the CIA significantly influenced activities in Laos. Premission briefings indicated that there were mobile training teams (MTTs) already operating in Laos. We understood that we could be of the greatest assistance by winning the hearts and minds of rice farmers, fishermen, and other local people.

### The Briefing

The morning of our background briefing on Laos bore all the makings of a beautiful late-summer day, the kind of day that makes you want to inhale nature's essence. Perhaps it was the kind of day that inspired Robert Browning to write: "God's in his Heaven and all's right with the world."

Although quite unlike the usual army facilities, the woodland setting typified the kind that a Special Forces operational team uses in an unconventional warfare area. As such, it was much better than the normal air-conditioned classroom.

After the previous mission to Vietnam, I hoped it would be a day when the briefing officer might utter these words: *Laos is a wonderful country for a mission and the highlands are a magnificent forested range of mountains. In their cracks and crevices flow beautiful rivers that drain the pleasant jungle. Most of the land where the people live is level. This is a wonderful place where you will live and work. You will enjoy yourselves all the time you are there.*

Almost as though it meant to warn us, the weather suddenly changed from sunny to a torrential downpour, forcing us to move the session into a regular classroom. The NCO's talk dampened our spirits even more. A bleak picture of the country emerged as he discussed Laos's climate, culture, enemy resistance elements, terrain features, logistics, religion, transportation, and airfields. We learned that malaria and malnutrition were prevalent. Life expectancy was low. Health care facilities were grossly inadequate.

The briefing officer described the position of Laos as a small, landlocked country located south of China, west of Vietnam, north of Cambodia, and east of Myanmar and Thailand. The capital of the country is Vientiane. Laos had—and has—one of the lowest per capita incomes in the world. Part of French Indochina after 1893, Laos was granted independence by France in 1953. After the French left, a prolonged civil war ensued. This allowed the Pathet Lao to move in and establish their own political and military presence, which we would attempt to upset. The NCO continued, "Your mission will live up to previous ones—challenging and dangerous. In this secret war, the casualties are high and the perils are appalling."

We were told that the population of Laos was indeed ethnically complex, with each ethnic group tied more closely to related groups outside the country's border than to the Laotian nation. The dominant group, the Laotians, accounted for nearly 55 percent of the total population. Most of them lived in the floodplains along the Mekong River valley and its tributaries. For our mission it was necessary to understand the ethnic mix of the rest of the Laotian population, 30 percent of which was the Lao Teung and 13 percent the Hmong and other hill tribes; the tribal Tai constituted another ethnic group. We learned about the agricultural methods of each group and its location in floodplain or mountainous terrain.

In a succeeding briefing, official agents told us that the CIA had advised the president and the National Security Council on developments in our area. According to them, in our "spare time" we were to report directly to them on international developments in Laos and other countries. We were to perform political, economic, technical, and military functions in areas that we considered important. The agents also told us that we might become directly involved in counterintelligence activities, that is, we would likely be called upon to monitor foreign radio broadcasts.

It was a lot of information to absorb about a tiny land-locked country that had achieved sovereignty only five years before. We had no inkling of the place Laos would take in the newspaper headlines of the future. We did know that in Laos our experience and character would be tested again to the utmost.

### More Bad News about Laos

As a protectorate of the French before World War II, Laos had served as a buffer state, shielding France's interests in northern Vietnam from Thailand and from the British in Burma. Familiarization classes made it clear to us that modern Laos—independent Laos—was engaged in vicious, take-no-prisoners internecine warfare.

We were thoroughly briefed on the history of Laos since World War II, when it was occupied by the Japanese. Like other former colonies of European nations, Laos developed strong nationalist intentions under Japanese occupation and did not welcome the return of the French, who were obliged to grant it independence in 1953.

By 1958 the communist Pathet Lao, trained and equipped by the Viet Minh, controlled the countryside, although not in the sense of wielding central power as a unified force. Laos's various regions were more or less autonomous, dominated by their respective ethnic populations. Area administrators effectively wielded more power than the military headquarters in Phen Tenh. The Laotian leadership was nominally lodged in the capital, but we would be dealing with the people's real leaders, in the countryside.

We learned that the Meo (Hmong) were from an ethnic background quite different from that of the regular Laotians. Unofficially, we would hear that our team, with the support of the CIA, was going to equip, arm, and train them. Subsequent official briefings informed us that the Meo were willing to resist communist aggression by any means necessary; and we were prepared to stay with them, lead them, and, if necessary, die with them.

### The Plan

Regardless of the mission, our ritual remained unchanged. First, we had to go through routine processing involving the preparation or updating of wills, powers of attorney, detailed records, personnel files, and payroll adjustments. Our entire pay and allowances were put into a bank account of our choice. Then, the whole team went into complete isolation while the operational plan evolved and advanced. Each of us learned by heart the many pieces of information, such as map readings, schedules, names of people in high places, and radio—particularly frequencies, which I could do with very little effort; they always came easily to me.

During isolation, we received final approval to execute the operation. Our official mission was called "Hotfoot"; we were to lead an irregular militia unit operating in the rural villages of Laos. As an MTT, we were officially civilian members of the Program Evaluation Office (PEO) and would work directly with it in building training sites and distributing new equipment. In addition, we would provide the Laotian troops with instruction in Special Forces counterinsurgency. The plan included making jumps whenever possible with our Laotian counterparts.

The mission was to be executed in Luang Prabang and in other locations near Vientiane, our future headquarters. Our team would assist the counter-revolutionary forces converging at Savannakhet. We would follow these troops into the field and advise them on combat operations. The team consisted of two officers, two senior NCOs, an intelligence NCO, two weapons NCOs, two medics, and two communications sergeants. We continued to operate as the 14th Special Forces Operational Detachment.

The operation was our version of a tactical operation order in a conventional unit. Since one of our major concerns was the availability of resources in the field, we took account of everything down to the last item. Although we would gather all available information from the briefings, orientation, and background study, we knew that everything could change by the time we reached Vientiane. Thus, we had to convince our commanders that, regardless of the circumstances, we could go into the conflict in Laos, complete our mission, and return. This was our supreme test.

Before leaving isolation we were, as always, completely "sterilized," that is, relieved of most maps, uniforms, correspondence, ID cards, or other forms of identification. We did receive an allowance to buy wash-and-wear civilian clothing.

## Typhoon

Before leaving Okinawa, our team got an opportunity to assist some of the local populace.

While on stand-down, we kept busy and alert by training in crucial operational techniques. There were many parachute proficiency jumps, additional escape, and evasion training.

We conducted a preoperation exercise near Futenma. We had arrived at an area, chosen on the spur of the moment two or three days earlier, and took refuge in an old, rather large building (an unused barn). On this particular night, we were reviewing Phase One training on patrolling, raids, and ambushes, including a refresher on techniques of exerting gradual physical, psychological, and other pressures on insurgents.

The air was calm and hot. As a team member was reviewing the basics of patrolling, low-hanging, dirty clouds appeared in the sullen sky.

"It's dark for afternoon," I remarked.

"Yeah! In addition, the air feels weird," he replied.

"Maybe we should radio headquarters."

However, we agreed that it was probably unnecessary and continued with a lesson on viewing conflict from a tactical level, that is, from subtle political and social perspectives. At this point in our training, we were fully aware of the complexity of effective conflict resolution. We had settled in to discuss some fundamental reasons for conflict, probing beneath the obvious motives dramatized by the media.

About an hour later, the sky took on an even more ominous look. A yellow shadow hovered overhead. The air became so chilly that goose bumps popped up on my arms. An unearthly calm settled over everything. Suddenly, the sky seemed to unzip and the rain crashed down upon us. The heavy downpour pounded the roof of our dwelling and shattered nearby windows. We knew that we were in for a rough time.

Someone turned on the voice radio to try to determine what was happening. Soon the news came.

"A typhoon went through a village near Futenma, tearing up everything in its path!"

There was announcement, followed immediately by a request for all available medical personnel to help with the injured and dying and for everyone else to stay away. The other medic and I stood at the ready to offer our help. Two hours later, we got our chance.

About dusk, an open-air, cattle-type truck filled with people crossed the bridge from Futenma and stopped in front of our building. We herded the shivering and bedraggled people inside. "These folks lost everything but their lives and the clothes on their backs," the driver shouted from the doorway.

"They've got no money, but they are hungry and need shelter. Can they stay here until I can go get another load?"

"We will handle it!" a team member yelled above the hammering rain.

Everyone scurried to make the storm victims as comfortable as possible. Shortly, we had the two old pot-bellied stoves going strong. We strung up a line to make space for a kitchen and cordoned off separate areas for people to hang wet clothes. We offered our spare clothes to the women. Moments later, the makeshift rooms were a maze of dripping dresses, trousers, shirts, and underwear.

We quickly transformed an old door with supports into a supper table. Two "scouts" left and returned with a small calf and other edibles.

We also prepared rice. Its abundance in Futenma ensured that there would be enough of some kind of food for everyone. Besides the rice and calf, we quickly spread hamburger patties from our C-rations across our Special Forces–type grill. Soon the aroma of onions, burgers, and chili mingled with the smell of wet hair and clothes.

As we served the food, a long-haired, extremely thin woman crumpled to the floor. When she refused food, we offered hot coffee, which she accepted. Her eyes stared blankly ahead.

"It sounded like a train bearing down on us," she muttered. "The whole side of my house exploded. The next minute, my mother was lying under a big pile—dead! Right besides me—dead! I am not scratched!"

Soon the truck returned from Futenma with another load of victims. Others continued to arrive in cars, wagons, trucks, and on foot until the building filled with sleeping men, women, and children. We stayed quite busy throughout the night.

The next morning, the people awoke to the smell of tea and coffee brewing. We served them eggs and bacon, rice, and a variety of breakfast food and C-rations. There was enough wood nearby to keep everyone warm and dry.

Understandably, the people were eager to return to their homes to try to salvage whatever they could. When the rain finally subsided to drizzle, they took it as a sign to begin their journey back home. The Special Forces headquarters group in Futenma set up temporary shelters and provided assistance.

Although the typhoon was a tragedy, our close association with the people during the crisis helped us to earn the respect of the local population. As on previous missions to Thailand, Taiwan, and Vietnam, we made friends for our country and our cause. Many of the people grew to appreciate and respect us for helping to forge international bonds of assistance and cooperation. By now we thoroughly understood how vital it was to cultivate goodwill among people who often harbored hostilities among themselves.

## Mission Hotfoot

Even now, almost four decades later, I still remember Laos as if it were the day of our arrival—the people, the jungle and its beauty. I also remember the jungle and its horrors, a jungle that never slept.

The year was 1959. Frustrated with the state of the _Armée Nationale de Laos,_ the Program Evaluation Office (PEO) entered into negotiations with the _Mission Militaire Française près du Gouvernement Royale Laos._ These negotiations resulted in an agreement allowing greater direct U.S. participation in Laotian training. Laos, as other countries worldwide, requested training from Special Forces mobile training teams (MTTs). Consequently, around the middle of the year, acting as civilian members of the PEO we arrived in Laos from the Royal Thai Air Force base in Udorn to conduct Mission Hotfoot. The "team" (a common expression for a Special Forces detachment of about twelve soldiers) prepared to live, work, and fight for six months as members of a Laotian army battalion.

Excitement ran high as we flew from the control center to the contact area. We could see very little of the countryside from inside the plane, although the pilot did his best in reporting our position. The small peepholes in the hot, stuffy interior of the aircraft were just large enough for us to get our bearings when the clouds permitted. We carefully followed the pilot's indications on our maps, noting when we passed over Paksane and Thaket. Even so, the navigator had to correct the course from time to time, as it was imperative that we get to the reception area on schedule.

Soon we emerged into the bright evening sunlight, leaving the clouds far behind us. However, darkness was now rapidly approaching. Although none of us dwelled on the fact that we would be without covering fire upon landing, we all breathed a sigh of relief when, just short of zero hour, we detected a "T" on the ground. This was the signal that it was safe to land. We were at the right place at the right time.

The pilot maneuvered the plane in a wide circle, searching the ground for the flat meadow our orders described as our landing strip. It never showed up; rather, we discovered that the terrain of the designated drop zone was alarmingly rough. Just the danger involved in setting the plane down could have ended the mission. We decided to go in anyway. To our relief, the landing proved to be uneventful.

I despised the area instantly. A narrow, winding five-mile-long dirt road stretched menacingly between the landing zone and our southerly destination in Laos. Lined on both sides with heavy rain forest, the road was an ideal setting for ambush. All of my old training instincts and Vietnam experiences came flooding back: the heightened awareness, the rush of adrenaline, the sense that we had to move quickly and decisively.

We moved out on foot the next morning. These were the cool, dry days of winter. The average temperature ranged between 20 degrees and 70 degrees Fahrenheit. Low clouds, barely three hundred feet above the valley floor, had moved in during the previous evening, adding to the morning mists that shrouded us as we trudged through the bamboo and scrub brush.

Ironically, despite the evident danger, I rather enjoyed the trek to the battalion area. The slow forward plod up and down the mountains, the calls of birds and whoops of monkeys ringing in my ears, induced a feeling of serenity. True, the danger of running into a patrol and a potential firefight traveled with us, but firefights were exciting. In addition, although I knew that I could die at any moment, I gave little credence to the possibility. Fortunately, pre-infiltration intelligence reports, indicating no current enemy activity in the area, held true.

While en route to the battalion area, word reached us of the destruction of a hamlet about ten miles due north of the camp near Muong and Savannahket. According to reports, no one survived. However, intelligence among the civilian population was excellent; and there was the possibility that the majority of the villagers had fled before the attack and not yet returned because of the enemy threat. Later, we learned that, while this was the deadliest single attack in recent months, such attacks were a common occurrence in this war-ravaged region. Its victims—men, women, and children—included the very old and the very young.

Along the way we saw many people seeking sanctuary, some riding ancient trucks piled with household goods, bicycles, and live animals. They had heard the news of the hamlet's destruction and knew they might be next.

We looked for and found the deserted hamlet. The enemy had burned most of the shacks. It was not hard to imagine the details of the village's death agony. Looking around at the corpses, I thought, "These people must have felt buried in bodies." Given our precarious situation, we did not take the time to count all of them, deciding to continue to the military staging area instead.

The Laotian battalion that we joined, patterned closely after an American airborne unit, had the strength of approximately five to six hundred soldiers. It consisted of five companies, rather than the usual three, and a number of additional attachments. Our first step was to determine the enemy's military location and strength nearby and in the area between the base and the destroyed village. As far as we could determine from information we received from the control center and other villages near the site, enemy activity had ceased for the time being. Therefore, at that point we turned our attention to helping the villagers. All of this was quite different from the responsibilities I had expected.

When we returned later to the village, some survivors had already come back. Colonel Madding and the Laotian commanding officer decided that one detachment would remain in the area for two days and help the villagers get back on their feet. As senior team medic, I would visit as often as needed with a small detachment of Laotians that we would train to help in restoring order to the village. (After only a few hours of instruction, they welcomed the opportunity to render aid.)

Since we were acutely aware that incidents such as this cruel and senseless crime could have international implications, we immediately radioed the details of our location and a description of the situation as we determined it to the control center in Okinawa.

The village must have been a lovely place at one time. Located a short distance up the side of the mountain, it appeared to be wrapped in a curious state of conflict and tranquillity. It also seemed caught in a time and culture warp, even for Laos. Devoid of telephones, its only contact with the outside world was a single telegraph line. The main highway nearest the village stretched approximately fifteen to twenty-nine kilometers over the worst terrain in that part of the world.

Evidently, many villagers died in their beds. Numerous bullet casings lay in the street. We found holes inside and outside of what appeared to be a temple, and on a fence post where they killed a community leader. On one street corner, we discovered a commemorative picture of a slain teacher. Reportedly, the enemy had executed him for no particular reason except to say to the rest of the village, "Here's what happens when you support the government." The enemy was no slouch in mutilating the dead and torturing the living. One account told of how they had taken a young villager into the center of the main square, broken his legs, and buried him alive.

We watched at a distance as the villagers solemnly transported the bodies of their neighbors on wood slabs or in hastily built boxes. Absolute silence permeated the entire village as the people walked across a bridge to the burial grounds and deposited the corpses.

Laotians, like most other cultures, are strict and meticulous about the treatment of their dead. They accord them the usual acts of respect, including interment in a particular place on home ground. When the mournful procession ended, 149 bodies lay side by side. Although we tried to remain impassive, I could not repress a shudder.

By the evening of our second day, we were back at the battalion camp, which consisted of a number of wooden and bamboo structures. There was even an officers' club of sorts, a structure consisting of a fairly large bamboo shack and several tents.

The depth and warmth of the camp inhabitants' welcome overwhelmed us. There were about seventy noncombatants in the camp, Laotian civilians who were mostly families of the soldiers. (The official count included noncommissioned officers, junior officers, and one interpreter provided by Control, in addition to two interpreters brought with us from headquarters.) Civilians also filled the scrubby woodlands nearby, stretching out in the shade of crude carts or cooking meals over open fires. The dishes they served for supper that first night included fried mudbugs (crawfish), groundhog stew, wild mushroom soup, and grilled fish. All were simply delicious!

We had expected to take part in local festivals and celebrations, participate in the battalion's battles, eat the local diet, and live mostly off the land. In addition, we had planned to help the local communities with their crops. In this respect, I anticipated using my farming experience and rural background. I also planned to develop a literacy program.

Unfortunately, because of the realities of the situations we came across in Laos, my plans for promoting education did not come to fruition. However, our efforts in providing medical assistance were tremendously successful. We instigated medical training and treatment for villagers as well as for the troops.

### Sizing Up the Situation

Secrecy enveloped much of what was going on around us. For one thing, the battalion was a segment of the Royal Laotian Army. Military action at this place and at this time could have far-reaching political consequences. Without a doubt, we needed to perform a thorough situation analysis immediately.

Communicating with Savannakhet was one of the top priorities of Operation Hotfoot. Both ends of the chain of command required clear, secure, and timely exchange of information. They had to know what was happening while it was happening. We needed to tell them what assistance we required—ammunition, medicine, food, etc.—as the mission developed. Although we could have used reinforcement, there was no chance of getting it.

Headquarters personnel considered themselves experts in determining the needs of teams in the field. However, I cannot recall them ever giving us direct orders. On occasion they made suggestions, but in the field we were completely on our own.

The radio operators were the technical hearts of the mission, and state-of-the-art secret gadgets were a standard part of their inventory. However, when necessary, they could rig the radios with almost anything. The "Angry 9" with a hand-cranked (G-43) generator was the radio of the day. Often improvisation of equipment took precedence over all other efforts. We erected antennas, tested generators, and switched on radios. A team member ground away on a generator while the radio operator keyed the most pressing situation message.

Our initial report on the evaluation of the total military and civilian circumstances went to Control on schedule. Since both the communications people and Control knew our timing and frequency level, the message reached its destination. Vientiane was on the line! Of course, so were listeners from the Soviet bloc. Although we had all sorts of devices for encoding, decoding, and condensing messages, communications security was a great concern. Whenever the communication team sent messages there was a chance that anybody could receive it and break the code.

### The Mission Evolves

That first night in camp we slept in makeshift bunkers, in sleeping bags, and rolled up in ponchos. It was around 4:00 A.M. when we turned in. We tried to get some rest before daybreak so that we could take a closer look at the circumstances unfolding around us. Although most of us probably would have preferred to be in the jungle in our hammocks, we still slept like rocks and woke up ready to go to work.

Because of our earlier assessment, we knew that there were few pieces of military real estate in Laos more valuable than this spot. The surrounding hills and tree-canopied jungle made it perfect terrain for our planned training activities.

Our orders were to teach guerrilla concepts for an undetermined period. We wanted the troops to avoid engagement with the enemy's main force units, fighting only when confident of quick and decisive victory. We wanted no other enemy contact except by ambush.

We drilled the Laotian troops on our basic tactical philosophy: "Shoot first and move first." In other words, in event of point, flank, or rear contact, they would swiftly develop fire superiority and immediately assault the enemy. If it turned out to be a small unit, one that we could dominate, we would overrun it. If we had to fight—lock horns with a large enemy force—we would break contact and get the hell out of there. Once contact was broken, we would speedily move back to our route of withdrawal. We had to know the game and we had to play it well, because in this game of life and death you lost only once.

From our briefings in Okinawa, we knew that this battalion was a CIA-conceived outfit, designed with United States military assistance to become a Special Forces type of operation. Under the direction of Allen Welsh Dulles, the agency engaged in a large number of undercover activities in Asia. Laos was just one such operation. The CIA viewed our team and its activities as a strong symbol of the American presence in "neutral" Laos. In other words, it needed any successes that we could deliver.

We reasoned that the agency's support would strengthen the battalion's defense stores as we radioed urgent needs and reports from the field. We needed loads of barbed wire, tons of cut timber, civilians to serve as "Seabee construction gangs," and funds to pay them. In the meantime, we had to make the best of whatever supplies, equipment, personnel, and funds we had on hand.

Providing enough uniforms for the soldiers presented a problem, too. They wore U.S.-issued OG 107 fatigues with appropriate rank and insignia. Unofficially, we wore military uniforms, often including the bush hat, as opposed to the usual civilian clothes. While we wore neither American unit insignia nor any other identifying insignia in the field, we did wear Thai and American parachute wings on our right and left breasts, respectively.

I wore OG 107 fatigues and my personal weapon, a custom .45 ACP (Automatic Colt Pistol) government model attached to an M155 pistol belt. I was never without this weapon of choice. All weapons worked flawlessly, despite frequent use.

Intelligence told us that the Pathet Lao had many unknown camps and complete freedom of movement within a wide territory of nominally government-controlled areas. Although we considered ourselves a tiny island of security within an ocean of desperate enemy, we were now knee-deep in their territory. While our camp closely resembled a simple military compound or battalion position, our immediate plans were to implant a blocking force at the juncture of enemy supply roads and trails.

We also introduced the concept of underground living. As in every war, good protection meant deep, hand-dug foxholes. Apparently, no one had considered digging trenches, filling sandbags, or concealing themselves in the already-constructed bunkers. (Perhaps they thought such actions would have been a waste of time.) In the future we would be certain to locate our control point for the airstrip and the battalion aid station underground.

We knew that we had to prepare adequate defenses immediately. The battalion's sergeant major informed us that the unit had not been on the offensive in any form or to any extent during recent months. The camp had a limited set of defenses, including mortars that operated from pits. It was apparent to us that the development of the art of defensive and offensive tactics was long overdue if we were going to survive.

### An Urgent Challenge

The battalion commander informed us of an impending 120-mm mortar barrage. He and his staff knew the approximate timing of the attack and the direction from which it would come because of intelligence reports from a variety of sources. He indicated that it would be accompanied by sporadic recoilless rifle fire and could go on for days. Soldiers commented that there would be "dead everywhere" afterwards. (Later, we found the attack as described; it was just one day in "many days of Hell" that we would experience.)

The attacks usually came every couple of weeks, according to the Laotian commander. At this point, we wondered about the battalion's intelligence sources. Knowing when we would be attacked was very useful, but we needed a great deal more general and specific information about the Pathet Lao and other matters.

At this point the situation was, without a doubt, an all-out conventional war. Forces whirling around us were coming to a head, and the outcome was anybody's guess. Therefore, we had to become major players in what happened next. By now, we fully realized that the battalion was in danger of destruction by the Pathet Lao. Although there were no actual threats now, the enemy was out there. Obviously, the commander understood the gravity of the situation, because he usually carried two or three M-59 grenades and an M-79 grenade launcher with him at all times. (As for me, aside from my Colt 45, I also frequently carried a U.S. M1A1 carbine or a submachine gun. I used the submachine gun if the occasion called for up to thirty rounds of rapid magazine fire.)

To varying degrees, our ongoing strategy dealt with such problems as fortification, maneuvers, and resupply. We had to know how many men were deployable, what kind of training they had had, and the state of their morale, as well as the number of available weapons. In addition, we had to consider the terrain and weather and the capability and location of the Pathet Lao.

Arming the soldiers and some part-time militia members was high on our priority list. The battalion's problems were now our problems, and the militia was one of the problems. Because militia members did not belong to the armed forces, police, or any other government security forces, there was always a special danger in dealing with them, especially the local ones. Word came to us that some of them wanted us killed. Also, we soon learned that ammunition, equipment, and supplies at the camp were running low. Some recipients of our dwindling stores might well use them against us.

Because our survival and the future of similar operations were on the line, our initial assigned role as multipliers, an advisory effort, had to take second priority. We observed that our reports could tremendously influence the role of future planning and execution of air and ground operations well beyond the scope of the battalion. Thus, the challenge was at once a combination of unconventional warfare training and conventional fighting.

On the night of our first major planning meeting, the sky lay black and flat, clamped like a lid of a coffin over the small tent we used. A complex picture emerged of what it took to preserve life now, as well as what would be required to fulfill our initial mission. The mixture of uncertain events occurring in the battalion, in the country, and in the world at that time required us to be prepared for virtually anything. Out of necessity, we had to persuade the commander to think "intelligence gathering," "offensive," "ambushes," and "patrols" as ongoing strategies. The commanding officer agreed completely with this assessment. It was primarily a matter of cultivating a positive attitude among them—and about them—a process that took time.

However, our immediate concern of the hour was defense, and its solution resulted from the input of the entire team. As usual, every team member participated fully in problem solving, leading by example according to his area of responsibility. For us, "leadership" meant working jointly. However, the team did not work on the problems alone. We worked with the commander and his staff in all decision making.

The planning and defense task forces comprised two or three of our team members, battalion members, and the commander and his selected staff. Granted, it took a while before battalion members could contribute to the extent of their abilities, because they lacked some kinds of experience. On the other hand, there is no substitute for the sort of training they got from being almost constantly in a kill-or-be-killed environment. We let them know that all of us could be creative.

In briefings, we pointed out the international implications of success and failure. These implications, of course, included consideration of the spouses and families of the soldiers, NCOs, and junior officers who, as dependents, often prepared meals for the troops. Our first task was to set up a stronghold as a partial camp protection. We needed machine guns set up to provide interlocking fire. Such weaponry could protect both the perimeter and the system of barbed-wire barriers. In addition, the plan called for soldiers and civilians to build trenches around the edges of the entire camp. The trenches, dug in a zigzag pattern to a depth of approximately five feet, connected the fighting positions and bunkers that also encircled the camp.

Because of the risk of injury to us by our own punji stakes, we firmly discouraged their use in ditches and trenches. We encouraged other defenses in the gullies. For example, the battalion's Claymores, exploding with hundreds of steel pellets, could cut a wide swath of death and destruction.

Immediately after the first officers' call upon our arrival (we requested NCO presence too), we began to work with the soldiers to start clearing a field of fire. At the same time, we constructed a landing zone consisting of an airstrip and a helicopter pad.

The next rather long-range step was to make the battalion the nucleus for Laotian Counterinsurgency Forces. The unit would possess the ability to conduct combined unconventional intelligence and commando operations in enemy-controlled areas and secret zones. A major plan was to use this camp as a model. We would work with the battalion in setting up similar ones. In due time, we also planned to assist the battalion in developing the capability to stab away at the evasive Pathet Lao networks, with small bands of its own trained security teams. At this point, though, we saw our ultimate goal as helping the troops to harass the communists and to slow them down as they tried to divide Laos.

### Conventional Preparation and Training

We began to work closely with the ANL building training facilities, distributing new equipment, and instructing the Laotians in counterinsurgency techniques. They agreed upon a credo for the battalion and the training program. It was: *Mighty enough to take on ten people; trained enough to teach an army.* Eventually, individual soldiers received a special mark of distinction with a special unit patch. Even the anticipation of receiving the patch helped to build esprit de corps. In addition, we promised them that we would work on authorization of an official snazzy headgear similar to ours. This idea proved to be a stroke of genius as a morale booster.

We were there to demonstrate, not to tell the commander what to do. We let them know from the beginning that our mission was to help them remain independent and evolve into a strong, unified, freedom-loving nation. Along with regular Special Forces practical directions, we told them that the way to happiness was to be able to decide their own fate. This included being able to live their lives with a minimum of outside interference (other than normal government controls). Our plan was not only to train the troops to train and fight directly but at the same time instill in them a sense of pride in their country and in the cause for which they were fighting.

The commander and troops were very positive and eager to learn. Our immediate assessment was that the unit's most pressing needs were for learning the art of leadership, building morale, and mastering combat basics. Since these activities required time, we assumed the initial position of indirect influence and support. Leadership and morale awareness came during our daily relationships and in the process of fulfilling the battalion's numerous military and other needs.

It was apparent that many of the soldiers needed training as if they were fresh from boot camp. For them, a desperate need was for basic infantry training. We had to prepare them to become fighters first. They had little experience with their weapons and even less with the fundamental military skills of patrolling. Medical training was almost nonexistent. We accepted these as routine Special Forces challenges, expecting that both the trainees and we would learn a great deal over the weeks to come.

Handicapped by a shortage of interpreters, we did our best to offer the young troopers practically the same type of training that had been given to us. Although we had to modify it because of time constraints, we managed to put them through the entire Special Forces qualification course on patrolling, raids, and ambushes. The course emphasized such operations as attacking the enemy's command centers; seizing airfields; and cutting roads, railways, and other lines of communication.

We kept all levels of the command informed of our progress. Our reports would directly affect their attitude regarding future MTTs sent to the area. We established a baseline of prevailing conditions, expecting to show encouraging improvements in subsequent reports. Considering that we started with a virtually undefended dirt track and a government counteroffensive that had yet to materialize, there would be much to compare.

We had to work quickly. In planning meetings, we determined that, while most of the soldiers knew nothing about immediate-action drills, they were ready to learn about security teams, watches, maneuvers, and fire. We would see to it that they learned. Fortunately, they were eager to learn. They needed to "live" the training each day.

We taught that bold attacks by small, highly trained groups could inflict great damage on enemy targets and morale. In addition, we urged them to work toward strategic reconnaissance capability, the penetration of enemy territory. What they needed was primarily conventional—Ranger-type—training. Other team members and I were ranger qualified, and that helped during certain phases.

Because the pending "next attack" was uppermost in our minds, we had to turn the tables on the attackers by making strong preparations for a defense. Our first order of business was to prepare a number of sandbags. Next, we had to locate packhorses and mules and to requisition ammunition and equipment through Savannakhet. We also had to physically inspect the grounds over which we would lead the troops during a major attack or an offensive effort. Airborne troops are supposed to be jump qualified, trained, and equipped to go into battle from the air, so as to bypass ground defenses and speed troops from staging areas to targets. However, the Laotian commanders preferred helicopters and tended to avoid any other type of airborne operations. At some point, we would be walking.

It was necessary to establish a major trail watch. We were able to convince the commander that these watches could serve as an important, effective intelligence network. Subsequently, with his cooperation, we contracted well-fortified road watch teams, positioned about one mile out in all four directions along the trails leading to the camp, establishing an outpost station on each one. Then, we set up forward monitoring posts overlooking the trails. Soon, the soldiers were quite busy preparing to fight, digging trenches and placing ammunition.

We and the Laotian forces soon developed tremendous mutual respect. Our mere presence seemed to boost esprit de corps. Like the nationalist troops in other countries, the Laotian soldiers were a willing bunch, bright-eyed and active. The question was, however, exactly where and how to direct this enthusiasm during certain military situations. We had a long way to go and would eventually experience a compendium of tactical errors and blown chances grotesque enough to break the heart of anyone who wanted to win a war.

### Inch Along, Walk, Airborne Shuffle

"Targets up!" yelled one of our team members, as small, straw-filled uniformed enemy dressed in black pajamas popped up downrange. The firefight that developed was innovative and relatively quiet. There was no accumulation of M1 rifle fire, no loud thumping of the M50 machine gun moved off to the left. Instead, we shouted a chorus of "bang -bangs" as the group moved forward in a series of coordinated charges.

This training exercise, on the front lines in Laos, might have appeared to be a humiliating consequence of inadequate funds. Rather, it was the first phase of an improvised emergency training process. Called "Inch Along, Walk, Airborne Shuffle," the training revolved around defensive tactics, strategic reconnaissance, and strike missions—not exactly part of our original mission mandate.

Since live ammunition was indeed scarce, we could not bring ourselves to use bullets for training purposes. Thus, after our team had walked along with representatives from the NCO and officer ranks, setting up and pointing out boundaries and stressing safety, trainees moved through the prepared lane with only shouted bullets: "Creep!" Next, following a detailed discussion and review to refine the efforts, the trainees began another "voice-fire" assault on the same objective. At this point, we ordered, "Walk!" Again, an after-action group reviewed and hammered out the Laotian troop's movement techniques. When the group was satisfied, the trainees repeated the exercise with . . . "Airborne Shuffle!"

This kind of exercise fit into the larger picture of the battalion's future military operations. We had to let the soldiers know that operational troops trained by Special Forces would need to deal with conflict, both military and political, as a philosophical issue as well as a physical challenge. At this point the focus was on their attitudes under stress, not their skills.

We needed to find out if we could turn this group of young individuals into leaders capable of defending themselves and their people. Our pledge—and immediate challenge to them and to ourselves—was to bring the battalion to the sharp edge of defense and counterterrorism. We also taught counterattacks and effective ways to reverse some of the initial setbacks experienced by the battalion. We worked long and as hard as necessary to accomplish our mission and did not tolerate mediocre training standards.

### Identifying the Enemy

Instruction in internal defense was also on the agenda. This facet of training, usually a peacetime variation of unconventional warfare (UW), was indeed one of the three basic missions of Special Forces. Although it was not in the battalion's original training plan, the situation dictated that it be conducted at this point.

We were in a strange phase of our "right then" war. The fact is that we never knew who the real enemy was. However, they knew us. The Pathet Lao's intelligence techniques were extremely effective. They knew the battalion's exact initial location and evidently had no problem pinpointing our precise spot on the map whenever we changed locations. Only enemy spies, operating within our battalion's ranks, made this level of intelligence possible. Soldiers told us that enemy soldiers and their spouses and children often washed and bathed in the same stream used by the *Battalion de Parachutistes*. Occasionally, our soldiers said, enemy troops waved to the battalion's troops in a friendly way. (We saw this ourselves, later on.)

We suspected one battalion of having in its ranks a number of Pathet Lao. Captured spies later revealed that they had developed maps by pacing off distances between the battalion's command posts, gun positions, and perimeter defenses. The enemy used these maps in preparation for assaults.

As a rule Laotian soldiers did not take prisoners; they executed known or suspected spies on the spot. Eventually, we were able to stop this cold-blooded practice during our tenure with the commandos. I assigned myself the task of discouraging it because I felt that it was wrong. I tried to convince the commanders and troops of the moral implications of killing human beings without a trial. Perhaps my Mississippi background, laced with reports of similarly brutal practices, directly influenced my reasoning. I felt confident that I would be successful in discouraging the practice because my requests to local troops carried almost as much weight as that of Colonel Madding, and I knew I had their respect. While I am not sure that the killing stopped (the scuttlebutt was that it continued to some extent), the troops did a good job of hiding it from me.

### One Attack of Many

For more than a month, the team had determinedly and frantically prepared our assigned Laotian soldiers for the day of the next communist attack. That day was now upon us.

Regarding the battalion's much-needed training, we felt that our efforts were successful. In the language of Special Forces operators, we had already "done good!" In just over a month, we had turned the troops' raw potential into a military capability. We had built up their bonds of camaraderie and had fine-tuned their resolve to be the best-trained troops ever.

In the process of training, we had deployed a number of troops for ambushes and similar tactics. They went out from the battalion base as parts of the unit's responsibility for keeping itself secure. This is where we ran into trouble.

That day I was with the small security group stationed about two meters southeast of the only bridge. We were near an area where we had detected the presence of a platoon believed to be part of a Pathet Lao main force. Not long after that, we sat in the sweltering afternoon heat with the enemy lobbing shells at us so regularly and unfailingly that we came to expect mortar rounds as a fact of life.

The Laotian commander ordered a detachment to come to our aid and to try to root the Pathet Lao out of the area. The detachment commander and I were to coordinate the operation. However, as team medic I still had to ensure the availability of medical treatment and supplies. "There appears to be enough plasma at the battalion to last through quite a battle," I remember thinking.

By the time the detachment arrived from the battalion, the enemy appeared to have withdrawn south down the road several hundred meters just north of the small river. We told the detachment commander that we were sure that a main force was nearby, preparing to attack the battalion. Our original plan—to move the troops down the road for two or three hundred meters and then face the enemy online—no longer seemed practical. Although our intention had been to trap them between our advance and the river, after quick deliberation the detachment commander and I decided that the most effective move would be to rejoin the battalion.

We had moved about seventy-five to a hundred meters out in the direction of the battalion area along a small dirt road when there was a sudden explosion about fifty meters ahead of us. (I surmised that a mortar round had detonated in a tree as the point element passed it.) For a moment, everything seemed to stand still. A strange-shaped cloud of gray smoke hung over the woods. In the sudden silence that followed, everybody remained completely motionless. The only things moving were the leaves that continued to shake. I shall never forget the curious peacefulness that settled over us for a second just before two individuals on the point collapsed.

My first obligation was to direct the care of the wounded. When I reached the first soldier, he was lying slightly off the road, with a tree limb on top of him. A stream of blood flowed from his mouth onto his chin and chest. There was nothing I could do. He was already dead. (Later, I determined that he died of a gastric hemorrhage.) The other individual also died instantly.

By then we were so close to the base that it seemed as if we could reach out and touch the bamboo shacks. Suddenly, we, the newly arrived American team, were again in the middle of hot combat. A rush of adrenaline shot through my body as a full-scale offensive on the battalion erupted. They hit us hard and fierce. The rattle and crackle of automatic weapons fire seemed to come from everywhere.

It came from our left front, from small bamboo huts, from a line of banana and other trees in the general direction of the battalion itself. Instantly, machine guns on the jungle side of the camp opened fire vigorously. Several persons directly in front of us crumpled to the ground.

A senior Laotian NCO was making his way to the front element. Earlier, I had wondered how the battalion commander would respond under an attack of this type. It appeared that we would soon know. The loud, shrill tweeting of a police whistle attested to the fact that he was alert and rallying his troops. We had established the use of whistles to signal commands. Hand and arm signals were useless in the jungle and, of course, voices did not carry over the noise of combat. One blast meant to deploy online; two meant to assault; and three meant to break contact and get the hell out of there. (The whistle, indeed, proved to be the most effective way to communicate commands during the conflict.)

After an hour or so of incoming fire, the chatter of machine guns from the battalion area died down to sporadic bursts. Then someone blurted out, "One more Pathet Lao wave coming!" Savagely the battalion's machine guns chopped at the jungle again. A whine of shrapnel came from somewhere. We dove for cover, scrambling for any means of protection we could find. Shells were landing everywhere. Soldiers lay huddled against the ground with their weapons at the ready.

Grateful for having stored ample ammunition, we continued to shoot into the jungle, but the enemy had ceased to return fire, once more an invisible threat.

Subsequently, we decided to flank the enemy and move around to the relative safety of the battalion. However, we desperately needed more protection. Waiting to move farther in the direction of the battalion area, I remembered similar scenes from films of the first and second world wars. There could be no denying that, for me, knowing what could happen was more frightening than ignorance or uncertainty.

We reached the battalion area, but mortar fire began to rain down on us in torrents. A soldier near me fell dead. Another blast almost severed both legs of a senior Laotian NCO whom I had come to know well and admire. Though gravely injured, he continued to yell words of encouragement to his comrades and platoon until unconsciousness overtook him. He died soon thereafter.

The mortar bombardment continued unabated for about forty-five minutes, obliterating most of the structures in the camp. Then the enemy stormed in from the north where we were deeply entrenched and quite able to turn them back. Slowed by the barbed wire and underbrush, they were easy prey for our rifle and machine gun fire. Launched almost straight up from the center of the camp, our mortars rained out along the wire. The attackers faltered briefly, re-formed, and charged. The battalion hit back hard. Finally, the enemy broke off the attack and fled. We did not pursue.

We captured three enemy soldiers that day. They were "wrapped inside" rolls of concertina wire as confinement. It was, of course, impossible to survive such severe conditions for long. The troops killed them after they served intelligence purposes. This was a traditional practice in Laos, as brutal as their treatment of spies. Another practice was to compel condemned persons to dig their graves. They were then shot in the right side of the head with a .45-caliber pistol; they fell or were pushed into the graves, and were immediately covered with dirt.

Taking the lives of captured enemy was not a matter for too much agonizing on their part. Still, we did not condone the practice of killing prisoners and tried to discourage it.

We discovered that the uniform of one captured soldier consisted of items taken from dead government troops, along with a Soviet-style tank crewman's helmet. Team members were certainly learning a lot about this particular war and the major parties who were fighting it. For us, this was somewhat of a new league. Despite what had happened already in Vietnam, from training to fierce, direct combat, we were beginning to wonder where it all would end—or perhaps we did not want to know.

Our defensive training proved to be successful in many ways, and we learned a great deal from the situation. The Laotian troops, civilians, and our team members exhibited astounding bravery. In my opinion, it was evident that the battalion segments, from the commander to civilians, certainly had the minds and makings to be great fighters.

### A Major Siege

A couple of days later, it rained about the middle of the afternoon, and by nightfall most of our ponchos were currently in place as tents. We were wet, cold, hungry, and exhausted from preparation against another enemy attack. The smell of death hung heavily in the air.

We dug in for the night in an outpost.

The battalion's and the team's primary concern was the defense of the camp. Maintaining the outposts, from which reconnoitering missions could deploy, was also important. Our paramount objective was to determine the enemy's location, the extent of his preparation for attacks, and his involvement in hostile activities. In addition, we set up a nighttime ambush to trap unsuspecting Pathet Lao. Although fresh troubles continually descended upon us, we told ourselves that things could have been much worse.

With our assistance, the commander and his staff had begun working out the details for an all-around defense. We made careful calculations of distances and determined the availability of arms and equipment that we would need at the time of an assault. Each company, each attachment, and other groups of soldiers received special assignments and were given instructions in exactly what they had to do.

We placed the main defense near the battalion's headquarters, close to the center of the encampment. The main defense also included a nearby fortified hilltop. This particular hilltop was one of the four outposts used for information gathering; it also contained a helicopter-landing pad.

A helicopter sent by headquarters shuttled between outposts and the main area whenever there came a break in the fog, incoming mortar barrages, and other airborne deliveries. The saying heard frequently in communications with the helicopters was, "Is the LZ [landing zone] clear?" (Sometimes pilots attempted to pick up the wounded from unsecured LZs, but few, if any, would try unless they knew the situation.) Our estimates indicated that there were from five hundred to a thousand communists in the jungle near Savannakhet. Also, according to our calculations, there were at least two battalions concealed in the distant surrounding mountains. It was reassuring to know that the camp was well fortified.

Our presence made the battalion's camp a particularly attractive target. However, the anticipated attack came much sooner than we expected, and it was a major siege. In a predawn probing attack that subjected us to 120-mm mortar barrages, sporadic recoilless rifle fire, heavy machine gun fire, and possibly a rocket launcher, we kept quite busy. Although the battalion's executive officer was young and new, he and one of his senior NCOs worked closely and effectively with our weapon person. The group organized what we believed to be an effective defense, pattern, and rate of fire that could chop away at advancing enemy.

Figuring there would be a heavier drain on ammunition and medical supplies than originally estimated, we radioed our assessment of the situation to Control. They informed us that there was no chance of artillery support or of immediate reinforcement. The unit's sole support would consist of a single Forward Air Control (FAC) aircraft and drops of food, when possible.

Control dispatched an aircraft to replenish the camp by parachute. However, the area was completely obscured by clouds, and some of the parachutes drifted beyond the perimeter. Two team members and two groups of soldiers managed to sneak through the elephant grass and retrieve nearly all the supplies. Their every movement seemed to draw rifle or machine gun fire from the Pathet Lao, who appeared to be regrouping for another assault. In the meantime, we evacuated most of the wounded to Savannakhet as another night of anxiety began. During this encounter twelve soldiers were killed immediately, nine were injured, and seven were evacuated or simply sent home.

Ironically, the assault had a side effect of developing camaraderie. We were beginning to know our battalion brothers-in-arms well. Friendships became richer by common sharing during training, preparation, and assaults. The simple act of dividing a can of fruit cocktail or a parched fish—tasting a few minutes of life in a trench with a person who was almost a stranger before the barrage began—made a difference in relationships. He became almost as close as a regular team member or a brother.

As we had been warned months before, casualties were high and the danger was indeed appalling for everyone in this "secret war." Together we watched Death roam among us. We accepted his choices, but still it was important that we all live to fight again, because there was much more at stake than our lives.

The training from Fort Bragg and Okinawa rose to sustain us. All of us, I believe, "felt" and trusted in the support and training of our fellow team members and were beginning to trust our new friends. Experience had taught us the significance of this rare quality. While we had some doubts about the loyalty of a few soldiers, never did the majority of Laotians (as far as we knew) speak of abandoning the hills and valleys to the enemy.

About this time, however, a situation arose that required some careful handling. A young soldier was exhibiting all the symptoms of rabies in its final stages. He had contracted it, evidently, from the bite of a young pet monkey. (The pet had already died and had been disposed of prior to our arrival.) Although medical manuals instructed us never to restrain patients, this situation dictated otherwise. Unable to do anything for him, we had him moved, in restraints, to the local hospital area, where he passed away. We could do no more than let him die where the dreadful course of the disease would not demoralize the other soldiers.

### And Still They Came

It was five o'clock in the morning when the enemy resumed the mortar attack of the previous night. This kind of war was survival in its rawest form. On our urging the soldiers dug deeper into the damp earth, piling more sandbags alongside their trenches. Whirlpool mists continued to coat us, and there appeared to be no escape. The real, full-time "Special Forces" challenge at this point was to keep the battalion's confidence and us all alive.

Seven Laotians were killed or wounded in their dugouts that day and fourteen evacuated. Thirty-nine Pathet Lao soldiers lay dead in the barbed wire around the foxholes and trenches. (I have the weapon that I captured during this particular clash. It is a submachine gun, without the round drum magazine.)

Later, when the team and a few of the battalion members were alone, we talked quietly about the battle, congratulating ourselves on a job well done. We were relieved to see that the Laotian troops were already beginning to develop "heart" and "spirit," becoming good at using many of the "saved" lessons acquired in training.

### Danger in the Jungle

The following morning we considered the new encampments of the Pathet Lao and Viet Minh, westward near Savannakhet, indicated by Intelligence.

The Laotian border is located in some of the most appalling terrain in Southeast Asia, rugged as the Rocky Mountains. Its steep ravines and valleys were breathtaking. Moreover, there was a lot of jungle out there. Fascinating jungle!

I remember that jungle vividly. Perhaps the world's most tense and dangerous area at the time, it was a scenic "no man's land." Everything being equal, the jungle would have been one of the most beautiful places in the world, if it were truly a peaceful place. Parts of it were spectacular. Deadly for humans, it was one of Asia's most hospitable homes for plants. Because of the monsoon season, the jungle stayed green year round. Thousands of wild purple aster, firs, pines, and aspens grew profusely, reminding me of the abundance of trees on my family's farm. Near some of the smaller villages, millions of beautiful red peppers were growing.

The jungle also seemed to be a refuge for cranes and a multitude of other kinds of endangered migratory birds and wildlife found almost exclusively in Laos. As the two factions battled across the approximately hundred-mile strip of land (a distance from about Baltimore to the outskirts of New York), swans and geese dove for food. The elegant cranes continued their strutting and preening, seemingly oblivious to the soldiers and equipment.

The bountiful nature of the jungle stirred up memories of the natural beauty of The Place, our family's farm, and the surrounding woodlands of the Mississippi hills. Looking at the sun haloed in rainbows over those lush green Laotian boughs, I marveled at the beauty and secret terror of the wilderness. Over here life was so cheap. Instant death lurked everywhere—death all around us.

I remember so well the day we were leaving the battalion area to go and look at a deserted enemy camp. We would stay for two or three days, so we took our rucksacks. I was commander that day and out front. The machine gun section and the rest of the team followed. Along with my Laotian counterpart, we decided to leave at least four men behind to serve as protectors from the rear.

Officially, we called this a "stay-behind and tail-gunner section." This section stayed in position for thirty minutes and ambushed any trackers who attempted to follow us. Farther away from the camp, we would use booby traps to discourage trackers, but while close to camp we did not want any of our people to stumble onto them.

As we threaded our way through the scrub brush, we thought about what we planned back at headquarters and about the map that we used to get ready for this expedition. In that map we placed pins to indicate where at least three battalions had been or might be at that time. The variously colored pins represented Pathet Lao (enemy) companies and platoons.

It was a beautiful day. The morning sun had burnt the mist from the mountains. Its warm rays felt good on my face. About thirty or forty meters from the base camp, we splashed across a knee-deep stream, passing a few thatched huts. For an instant, my mind again "journeyed back home," as my elders would say, to scenes both pleasant and unpleasant. Back to the one- and two-room shanties occupied by many of Tchula's black citizens. Back to memories of my childhood.

The stream's fast-moving, white sparkling water flowing over the smooth dark brown rocks in the creek reminded me of the creek that ran alongside our farm later on, in Lexington. Sitting on the front porch during those hot summer nights, welcoming anyone who happened to come down the road. Night teeming with the sights and sounds of life. Lightning bugs glowing brightly and then vanishing quickly from sight. The dew bathing the lush green lawn with refreshing moisture. The occasional breeze gently rustling through the magnolia, locust, and elm trees surrounding the house. The security of knowing that we could sleep with our doors open and no harm would likely come to us because of the community's closeness. Safe in the embrace of that community, we knew we would be all right.

In the Laotian jungle, I could feel the Invisible Hand upon my shoulders, urging me on, reminding me of the lessons that my family taught me about surviving in a hostile environment, just as applicable here in the jungle.

On the other side of the stream lay a silent domain of rubber trees that appeared planted because they were evenly spaced. (Our understanding was that no one had collected rubber for years, but rubber juice bowls were still visible everywhere.) We walked a little faster.

We were now well out into the area that we considered the war zone, where the Pathet Lao ran free. In fact, it was possibly the jump-off point for their attacks against us. About fifty meters to our right, we spotted a red clay surface on the northern trail, clearly marked on our maps. Of course, we did not dare walk down it because of its potential punji sticks and land mines.

Leaving the rubber trees behind, we proceeded downhill through a sunny area of bamboo trees, some as large as a foot or more in diameter. At the bottom of the hill lay a shallow stream of stagnant water covered with a crust of green algae. From a distance, the rancid odor of decaying flesh made it difficult to breathe. Upon further investigation, we discovered the partially decomposed body of a large dead animal. Huge, blue-green flies, so prevalent in Laos, swarmed around it.

As we moved past some fallen trees and large ferns, suddenly I saw a movement to the right of my head. Turning, I found myself face to face with a lime green snake with large yellow eyes. It stretched out across a couple of branches. I knew about snakes. Back in Mississippi, we have swamps filled with snakes. I was not taking any chances.

Instinctively, I slashed the snake across the head with the barrel of my carbine. When it hit the ground, I stomped the head into the dirt. The remainder of its body continued to whip back and forth furiously. My heart pounded frantically. Suddenly, someone yelled "Bamboo viper!" as one of the men dashed forward and cut it in half with his machete. Gazing from me to the dead viper, he breathed, "One bite from that sucker and you were going home in a box!" One enemy disposed of; the others—out there, somewhere.

We resumed our trek, eventually reaching the bright clearing we were looking for. In it stood a deserted building, one of a dozen or so thatch and bamboo huts. The grass was knee high.

### Jungle Survival

The terrain in Laos was similar to that of other countries in which we had conducted operations. The deep, cold, dark foreboding forest; the often rainy, grim weather; and the blistering days were reminiscent of Vietnam. But Laos was somehow more terrible, both in the beauty of its awesome scenery and in its deadly threats to life—the Pathet Lao, the poisonous creatures, the constant exposure to injury and disease. Bouts with malaria, hepatitis, and dysentery combined to make it extremely difficult for anyone to survive this strange war.

Our farm back home in Tchula had some serious swamps, filled with snakes, lizards, spiders, and, some folks said, even alligators, but they were kiddie wading pools compared to the jungles here. Surprisingly, we had little trouble with snakes other than the incident just described. But we would return from trips into the jungle and find big welts resembling blueberries on parts of our bodies—leeches! These vile creatures have blood spouts that contain an anticoagulant; once you began to bleed, it takes a while for the bleeding to stop. We saw soldiers wringing out their socks, completely saturated with blood.

In my opinion, the leeches were the most exasperating things about the trips through the steaming jungles. Resembling little wiggly worms, they would scurry rapidly across the ground to latch onto us whenever we stopped to take a break. One type of indigenous leech would stick to the leaves and branches of trees; and when they detected even a slight disturbance below, these little pests would drop down around our necks and quickly overrun the rest of our bodies.

Other types, once their little brothers and sisters had drawn "first blood," would detect it by smell and converge on their victims from all locations, dropping from branches and small bushes or scampering along the ground. Still other types lived in the water in schools. If you happened to step into a pool of those babies without protection, you were in trouble!

The leeches would look for any openings they could find in our uniforms. Usually they found none, because we knew from experience how to prevent them from getting next to our skin. We would cover boot tops, waistbands, flies, and sleeve openings; and we used leech repellent. (This repellent would be one of the first items requested from Control for the rest of the troops.) We always shared the repellent as long as it lasted. When our preventive measures failed, we removed the leeches by touching them with some type of hot object, usually a cigarette.

Because the jungle never slept, we had to maintain a constant vigil. Even within a short distance of the battalion area, our lives were in great danger. The last few days, in particular, had been a matter of life or death for all of us. However, we had trained well for situations of this sort; and we understood the jungle as well as anyone could who had not grown up there.

The jungle's foliage, three or four rain-forest tiers deep, concealed most of the camp's activities from aerial surveillance. It also rendered some of the artillery shelling and aerial bombing ineffective, often causing bombs and shells to detonate among the upper branches.

We marked the course of a rather large stream far below by the fog rising off the slow-moving water. Apparently, this spot would be the jumping off area for large-scale attacks spearheading the communists' movement against the country's government-held territory.

After about five months of our training and influence, each Laotian officer and NCO, as well as many of the men, adopted a distinctly theatrical swagger and fondness for exaggeration. I always carried a swagger stick (usually carved from local resources), and most officers and NCOs began doing the same. They walked with their heads held high, with well-deserved pride and obvious self-admiration. However, the Laotians transcended the theatrical to become highly disciplined soldiers.

Our six-month stint was over, and we would soon withdraw, leaving the Laotians to carry on. Little did we know that circumstances beyond our control would require us to return to Laos all too soon.

## Mission White Star

In 1961 the Royalists, with the growing approval of the United States, amassed their forces in the southern town of Savannakhet and prepared for a counterattack on Vientiane.

According to my notes, in 1961 the Program Evaluation Office (PEO) was renamed the U.S. Military Advisory and Assistance Group, Laos (MAAG), and the field training teams were renamed "White Star" mobile training teams. Thus, on 3 October 1961, about twenty-four months after completing Mission Hotfoot and a number of interim training missions, our Special Forces unit returned to Laos as Operation White Star.

Our orders listed six team members: Chalmers Archer Jr., James R. Daniel, Gene W. Hunt, Henry M. Jackson, Bruce B. McDonough, and George W. Snow. We would be in Laos—specifically, Bolovens Plateau, Nong Met and Camp Chanaimo, Vientiane, between 3 October 1961 and 4 January 1962. Our parent unit was the 7th Special Forces Group (Airborne), Fort Bragg, North Carolina.

The *Groupement Mobile* (GM) (the French equivalent of a regimental combat group) commanders of the Royal Laotian Army (RLA) had grown significantly in power since our last trip; we felt that they often approached the previously unchallenged influence of the military regional commander. Renamed Forces Armées du Royaume, the Laotian army was the primary force tasked with the defense of Laos at the time. Assigned to a *Battalion de Parachutistes,* we went directly into the field with them. Despite a nationwide orientation, in practice each GM remained in a specific military region. The same held true for the voluntary battalions in our vicinity. These battalions remained, I believe, active until around 1965.

As a unit, we suggested to the commander that they establish a mission for Special Forces in Laos. The main goals:

(1) Under the direction of the Laotian government, to plan, prepare for, deploy, and conduct unconventional warfare in any of its forms—guerrilla warfare, escape and evasion, subversion, and sabotage;

(2) to train Laotian forces in internal defense; and

(3) to perform special reconnaissance and direct actions in support of the government's national policy and objectives within designated areas of responsibility.

Our team's mission was to provide advice on comprehensive combat and other operations and to help raise unconventional forces among the Lao Theung tribesmen on the Bolovens Plateau and among the Hmong hill tribes in the north. Although we would be involved in a number of small skirmishes and some major battles, our overall objectives were to teach the Laotians how to shoot, build, farm, care for the sick and wounded, and run agent operations. Within the whole context of the Laotian conflict, ours was a relatively small operation in terms of size and cost. However, it contained the germ of early counterinsurgency and became a large part of the Laotian story.

As it turned out, the pattern of the war in Laos and our team's involvement would undergo continual change. As a Special Forces detachment of only six people, we found ourselves executing a number of different roles and missions. Consequently, we became involved in every conceivable aspect of counterinsurgency, straight military operations, economics, psychological operations, and even indirect political influence.

### The Civilian Imperative

Far eclipsing our Special Forces activities in both size and scope was the so-called civilian involvement, with its support of the battalion that we had taken on.

I thought of the battalion area, including the civilian component, as a camp—a well-protected area. With our help, the area became well fortified. We were deeply involved in carving that isolated camp out of the jungle and in keeping its floodplain area out of the Mekong Delta floods. We would be reporting to headquarters in Savannakhet.

Savannakhet, one of the larger cities, is located in southern Laos. The area around it (within a fifty-mile radius and as far down as Ban Bak) was a dangerous vacuum, one of the most ferocious battlegrounds in Laos.

Immediately upon arriving in the vicinity, we received a report about Maung Phin, a medium-sized town. For more than three and a half years, the farmers and laborers of this mountain village (numbering anywhere from two hundred to five hundred) had lived in a no-man's land. They were trapped between the forces of the Laotian government and those of the Pathet Lao and Viet Minh. (Perhaps the United States and our allies did not realize that the Viet Minh were still active in the area when we went there. That's the impression I received then, and it has not changed over the years.)

The villagers told us that the Pathet Lao had come to Maung Phin on a chilly night the previous fall, demanding provisions. In addition, they made statements that U.S. forces were fighting for the government and that the government was against God. A rather youthful-looking villager related the story.

One night his family was asleep inside their simple walled compound when someone knocked on the door.

"You have a son who is in the army," a rough voice declared.

The villager's mother asked, "What do you want with him?"

"He's an atheist who serves the government. Let us in!" they replied.

"No! No! No! You can't come in!" she shrieked.

A moment later, men armed with shotguns and long knives climbed over the wall. Two of them grabbed his mother, forcing her to her knees, while a third man stepped forward and slit her throat. Groggy with sleep, his father and brother stumbled into the courtyard only to meet the same fate.

The young villager was positive that he would die next. Instead, the enemy left him standing in the midst of his family's bodies. Clearly the guerrillas' intention was for him to spread the news of these horrible acts as a means of frightening the inhabitants of this and other villages into staying in line.

We learned that similar horrors did, in fact, occur all around Savannakhet that night as the Pathet Lao stormed house after house, brandishing a list which, they alleged, contained the names of everyone having even the remotest connection to the government. By dawn, an estimated fifty-six villagers had died.

I visited the town of Saravan. Its sunlit landscape of gardens and olive groves was deceptively peaceful. Earlier, the area was a center of savage fighting between government forces and the enemy.

During a visit to Chavan, a village near Saravan, I learned that thirty-six men had died a few weeks earlier when the Pathet Lao detonated a car bomb near a café. When I asked one of the villagers what was his greatest wish, he responded, "For peace and not to be decapitated."

In the area of the Bolovens Plateau, quite close to Saravan, I witnessed the results of even more nauseating atrocities. (In my mind's eye, the scene is just as vivid today as it was all those years ago.) I watched bloated and horribly discolored bodies float down the river toward Vapikhame. They were the victims of genocide from across the river. Their killers, the Viet Minh, were working too rapidly to allow for proper burials. Most of the bodies were completely naked. Some were missing hands or a head; others had their hands tied behind their backs. I could not take my eyes off one, a body that looked like a small doll.

Troops stationed in the area told me that this ghastly parade had been going on for a couple of days. The swirling currents near the top of the falls caused the bodies to speed up and hurl over, crashing down on the rocks below. It was awful!

This horrific scene convinced me beyond any doubt that these people had an undeniable right to maintain their determination and their hope of eradicating such evil. I could readily see why they despised the forces that had stripped them of their dignity and even their lives. I empathized with the pain and suffering of helpless civilians—as I do now, seeing on television the slaughter that goes on in other countries.

The Laotian forces we worked with may have also committed serious human rights violations. In 1961 the new leaders of the Laotian government attempted land reform, trying to convert village farms into more productive agricultural units; these efforts were not welcome in every instance. Moreover, there were reports of widespread corruption. We often heard that the ballooning foreign debt fed anti-Western feelings, and, in some cases, the government's determination to win the conflict led to cruelties that rivaled those of the enemy. For instance, the villagers in Chavan talked about the "advantaged people" who had resisted the government and had vanished without a trace.

The Laotians showed me thick binders containing snapshots of doctors, lawyers, teachers, students, taxi drivers, nurses, airline pilots, and others (teenagers and adults ranging in age from about fifteen to sixty-five) who they suspected were dead. An elderly civilian in the battalion area learned the fate of his two sons who had died in government custody. A Pathet Lao defector confirmed that the brothers had been confined with other prisoners in a stifling hot cell so cramped that only two could squat at a time, without water, food, or toilet facilities.

According to government reports, such incidents were "extrajudicial killings" carried out by the local equivalent of secret police. However, the fact remains that the Royal Lao forces arbitrarily arrested many of those suspected of involvement with the enemy and were responsible for a number of abuses, disappearances, and torture of detainees.

As despicable as such incidents were, however, the cruelest conflicts in recent history occurred before 1961. It is impossible to estimate the number of casualties, most of whom were civilians. According to reports, the Pathet Lao and Viet Minh fought with extreme savagery. They assassinated officials, writers, journalists, musicians, and anyone else whom they suspected of connection with the government. (All of this foreshadowed later happenings in Cambodia.)

The enemy spread propaganda about the ill effects of Western values. In retaliation, they destroyed over three hundred schools and murdered hundreds of teachers. They even slit the throats of schoolgirls who they claimed were not living up to the precepts of the local fundamentalist religion, which was either Buddhism or Taoism.

Despite these and other atrocities, the villagers who identified with us "refused to give up the fight," as one woman said. "I believe that it's better to be afraid while fighting than to do nothing at all," she added. "Besides," she continued, "I have a responsibility. We must put aside our fear and keep working for peace."

These villagers, like so many other ordinary indigenous people, suffered some of the worst acts that people can commit. Yet, they clung to their optimism, their hope, their fierce determination to withstand, their dreams of freedom. They were willing to battle seemingly insurmountable odds in their quest to regain it.

The people embodied the values of heroism, honor, dignity, and bravery that we often hear about but seldom witness. Yet, while I admired the civilians' determination, in the yards of those desolate villages the future of Laos seemed far from assured. We knew that somewhere the enemy fingered his weapons, perhaps hoping, as we were, that this war would soon be over.

None of these actions—of the enemy or the government forces—were widely publicized. In other words, the rest of the world paid little attention to Laos's troubles. No one knew what was happening. This was truly a secret war.

## "Winning the Hearts and Minds of the People"

The prevailing philosophy of many of our American forces and allies during this second mission to Laos was "bomb them back to the Stone Age"—kill all of the communist insurgents or incapacitate them to such an extent that they could accept any conditions. Contrarily, our Special Forces team knew that this stance did not take two fundamental considerations into account:

1. Most civilized people, including well-informed military people, are not willing to take such extreme measures; and

2. Past experience had proved that this type of approach simply does not work in the long run.

We predicted that any real chances for success in Laos (and Vietnam and elsewhere) would depend upon the counterinsurgents' ability to strike at the roots of the population's dissatisfaction. Those roots were quite evident. Extreme poverty existed side by side with extreme wealth. Corruption in government, unfair taxation, and high inflation ran amok. Health care, as far as we knew, was nonexistent. All the revolutionary authorities needed to do was exploit these problems by promising the people alternative leadership options in the future. Their persuasive arguments made counterinsurgency extremely difficult.

Consequently, if the government were to prevail, we had to demonstrate progress in the correction of the people's grievances. We had to act rapidly enough and effectively enough to wrench the initiative from the insurgents. We could not allow corruption to take credit for any changes for the better. It was a real Catch 22! Active fighting had already begun, making it virtually impossible to deal with the civilians' problems immediately.

Initially, the Pathet Lao and the Viet Minh concentrated their activities in the rural areas. We saw evidence that propaganda, revolutionary organizations, and terrorist tactics were bringing many of the villagers under their control. However, working closely with the CIA we learned that the majority of the "peasant" population was not committed to either side. They simply wanted to survive and live in peace.

We continued to work at winning acceptance and approval from the civilians. For example, we undertook civic projects in which we helped build schools, provided instructions and directions on building hospitals, and gave advice on building local government facilities. We also provided medical care. Because of some of our efforts, we were able to attract support from the civilian population almost anywhere we went.

### Equipment and Uniforms

Sources in the United States supplied all the equipment used during the White Star mission. The M-2 carbine was the standard weapon. Other equipment included the .30 caliber M-1 rifle, French MAS 36 rifles, the .45 caliber Thompson and M-3 "Grease Gun" submachine guns, the magazine bandolier, the M-1956 web gear, a lightweight tropical rucksack, and a steel helmet. Each battalion had 60- and 81-mm mortars, M-60 machine guns, and Browning Automatic Rifles (BAR). Heavy weapons companies had bazookas and 4.2-inch mortars.

Our uniforms reflected civilian status. Sometimes we wore nondescript fatigues without insignia, although we did wear our ties and military wings. Nonetheless, we adhered to an unwritten understanding that we would get rid of those in case of an emergency.

In the field, the Pathet Lao were heavily armed guerrilla forces representing conventional armor, artillery, and air force units. Both they and the Viet Minh acquired their equipment and uniforms mainly from Chinese and Vietnamese sources, although the Soviet presence was quite evident. For instance, from one captured Pathet Lao officer, I took a Soviet RDG hand grenade and a Soviet 7.62-mm SKS rifle with a folded scope.

The typical Pathet Lao officer wore a green shirt and trousers, standard apparel for the regulars during the 1960s. The headgear was a soft dark green cap with black leather visor and strap, and gold buttons. Privileged officers wore combat shoes with rubber soles, while those in the lower echelons wore rubber sandals. Often worn across the shoulders of officers was a brown leather map case. Often there were ballpoint pens displayed prominently in their shirt pockets. This was an additional status symbol.

PL regional forces and the village militia comprised slightly less than half of the enemy's total force structure. The PL supplied the civilian force with olive drab pants and khaki field caps. However, a captured member of the regional forces wore a khaki shirt with two pockets and exposed plastic buttons, commonly known as an "export" and considered a sign of privilege. The North Vietnamese supplied both the Pathet Lao and the Viet Minh with these uniforms. Many of these regionals owned Soviet AK-47 rifles and Soviet 7.62 Tokanev pistols.

During the 1960s, we trained several commando raider units in Laos for specialized behind-the-lines missions. This included prisoner-of-war rescue, cross-border raids, reconnaissance, and crisis site recovery. A team operating from our location in roughly northeast Laos occasionally wore North Vietnamese uniforms and carried SKSs. Sometimes they wore Pathet Lao uniforms while operating along what was later known as the Ho Chi Minh Trail.

Some of the weaponry that we provided for these units included the 2.75-inch rocket launcher. We improvised several versions of this launcher. For instance, we fitted highly explosive heads in a simple tripod attached to the launching tool. These missiles extended into North Vietnam, making it possible for us to harass troops in what the communists had previously considered "safe" territory.

The road watch teams (established along the trails during Mission Hotfoot) were now effective intelligence networks extending from the Nape Pass in the northern panhandle down to the Cambodian border. The teams instantly alerted air power to targets along the Trail. (The concept evolved to its highest level in the mid-1960s when we improved communications with radio gear. This improvement allowed the teams to relay their information directly to a processing center at an air base in Nakhonphanom, Thailand.) Most of them carried an M-2 carbine, the American standard. However, some of the teams carried the .45 Cal Grease guns.

### Six Men, Many Roles

In earlier missions the original members of the 14th Special Forces Operational Detachment had stayed together during numerous missions and had become cadre for the 1st Special Forces Group on Okinawa. Operation White Star was different in that team members served with operational units different from their original groups.

Mission Hotfoot, a previous mission in Laos, was as the 14th Special Forces Operational Detachment. However, the team for White Star was completely new to me. In addition, since there were now only six team members serving in an operational area, as opposed to the usual fourteen on some previous missions, we all had to wear a number of hats. One of my responsibilities was that of marksmanship trainer.

We continued to squeeze a great deal of training into six short months. We knew that effective training could save many lives and have positive international implications. In these future Special Forces soldiers, we sensed a determination to be among the best of their army. Our immediate goal was to prepare them to be ready for any contingency, nationally or internationally. This included jungle warfare and even desert warfare training, among other things. The ultimate objective was for the trainees to become capable of teaching Special Forces skills to others. This was true whether soldiers of the host country, soldiers of other countries, or civilians.

We trained the paratroopers in groups of three, focusing on each of the five Special Forces functional areas: (1) weapons; (2) construction/demolition; (3) intel/operations; (4) field first aid and preventive medicine; and (5) communications, operations, and intelligence. In addition, we planned training in underwater operations, parachuting, introduction to languages of adjacent countries, and jungle warfare. The trainees taught us a great deal about jungle warfare, but we also had much to offer in this area because we approached it as a science. Regardless of the specific area under consideration, we emphasized the concepts of intelligence, reaction time, physical fitness, strength, leadership, and willpower. We placed a heavy emphasis on willpower.

We also concentrated on first aid and medical treatment, essential preparation for armed combat. Equally important was the care of vehicles; a team member instructed trainees in preventive maintenance and simple repairs. Although we gave our trainees instruction about gunnery, they were already quite proficient in this area. Gunnery training was primarily the responsibility of the weapons sergeant. We did considerable training and cross-training in demolitions and firearms, two of my support specialties. I was especially adept with the pistol, handgun, and M-1 and M-2 rifles.

Usually trainees received quite a bit of instruction in military theory from the operations and intelligence sergeants. They attended rather extensive classes on small unit tactics. An area of major emphasis was the unit's leadership structure. The new teams consisted of twelve members, with ideally a captain in charge, although in our case it was often a lieutenant, with noncommissioned officers as the rest of the team. (Rank was relative; in any event team members had to be at least of noncom rank.) We let the trainees know that structure clearly delineated which member had overall and specific responsibility for the team.

In addition, we provided a limited amount of training in direct combat action operations (conventional tactics), similar to ranger training. Nevertheless, we communicated how important it was that they not make this concentration their primary focus. We also trained them to become masters of light infantry operations, which could also be a part of Special Forces missions. The purpose of these strategies was to temporarily seize and secure essential objectives.

### Sniper Training on a Shoestring

Important areas of extensive focus were sniper training, modified ranger training, and some pathfinder training. We also concentrated on patrolling, raids, ambushes, linkups, guerrilla-based security, and breakouts. However, the colonel who commanded this particular battalion determined that sniper training was the most critical need at the time.

We made it clear that there was no substitute for long hours under the watchful eye of a competent rifle instructor in becoming a marksman. I was the "king shot," or the outstanding sharpshooter on the team. I had also served as captain of the small bow and rifle teams. I happen to be a naturally gifted marksman; for that reason I had taught marksmanship in our detachment in Hawaii and the U.S. mainland and was a natural choice to teach marksmanship in Laos. For marksmanship training I had two assistant instructors, who were experienced sergeants, and an officer from the host battalion.

Some of our team members were already good shots but had never had formal sniper training; their competence and expertise rapidly developed under training.

### Marksmanship Training

The day before the marksmanship training began, I had had a conversation with the colonel that dominated my thoughts into the evening. He had stressed the importance of marksmanship training, impressing me with the seriousness of my job as a trainer.

I thought about that as I applied fresh mosquito repellent and prepared to settle into my hammock for the night. I remember how the once bright colors of the jungle became dull shades of gray. Low hanging storm clouds blanketed the area, blocking out the light of the moon and stars. Moisture impregnated the cold air of this monsoon night. Except for the intermittent flashes of lightning, the jungle was virtually black.

The next morning I awoke to the distant rumble of thunder as heavy rain worked its way through the canopy of trees and drummed noisily on my poncho stretched tightly above me. Raising my head, I looked over the side of the hammock. The distinctive smell of rotting vegetation assailed my nose as recollections from the previous day's activities crowded my mind. "Rain or no rain," I thought, "it's time to get up and get organized." The training cycle would begin.

The commander, sergeant major, and I had formulated the basic criteria for the class. We had determined that the "distance sharpshooter"—our term for a sniper—candidates should be members of the battalion who had shown exceptional skill with the rifle. It didn't matter how these individuals had acquired their skill; they could have been using a weapon in extensive hunting, prior military combat, or otherwise.

Fitness, however, did matter. I emphasized that a sniper must be in excellent physical condition. He had to be able to run, climb, or rappel, usually while carrying a heavier weapon besides his regular equipment. I told the commander and sergeant major that a good distance sharpshooter must have a strong heart and lungs. If a sniper's heart is racing or he is short of breath after a difficult climb up a mountain, he will not be able to shoot accurately. If his heart and lungs are sound, controlling his heartbeat and breathing is a matter of "keeping cool," as the expression goes.

Not surprisingly, many of the soldiers failed to meet all of the guidelines. Of the ten individuals selected from the battalion, none had any experience with the center fire rifle, a precision weapon we especially requested. The sergeant major also assigned me several overweight soldiers, whom I sent back, explaining that they could not keep up with the younger and more physically fit members of Special Forces teams. I determined that although I had some poorly selected individuals, I would not let the training degenerate into a basic rifle class. There was a time and place for me to conduct such a class, but this one was strictly sniper training.

One of my responsibilities as trainer was to conduct the briefing session. Basically, I assured them that they would be damn good shooters after the training—or else! I told them, through interpreters, that when they finished this training they would be a breed apart—not just good shots but among the world's best unconventional warfare experts. They would be expected to mature tremendously in the coming months and we would make sure that they did.

They had to understand, also, that they were being trained to become trainers; they were teachers first, warriors second. Knowing when to distinguish between those roles would demand some ingenuity, on occasion; combat conditions might be unique, unpredictable in every sense. No textbook would be able to help them.

As Special Forces sergeants and officers, they had to be experts in their individual areas of responsibility and in any other related duties or specialties essential to the Special Forces' many far-reaching missions.

I told them, as best I could, "You have a special role to play because you will be able to operate in your country or in other countries where conventional troops are inappropriate, unfeasible, or just plain inadvisable. Often, as Special Forces operatives you may be able to prevent conventional war and virtually save thousands and thousands of lives."

In the next five and one-half months, they would be trained to lead high-level military organizations. Our objective was to prepare them to take strategic or technical targets in pursuit of official, economic, or personal objectives in periods of peace or hostility. They went into the training knowing that they would have to uphold Special Forces traditions, and that only the most technically proficient and highly motivated senior NCO and officers would become Special Forces operators.

We conducted basic sniper training in one-week increments. The topics included examination of the role of a sniper, rifle and equipment selection, rifle preparation, and shot zeroing (adjusting the sights on their weapons). All were extremely important skills. This training also covered communication between the rest of the battalion and the sniper. In addition, topics covered basic marksmanship, low-light shooting, sniper tactics, location selection, shot placement (a bit distasteful to teach, but necessary), simultaneous fire, and basic ambush fire.

The sniper training also included sniper-initiated assaults, observances, and intelligence. Trainees learned to maintain a keenly observant mind, observe effectively, and interpret observations.

From the beginning, we took a realistic approach to the training, starting with the hundred-yard rifle range that the trainees constructed.

We briefly discussed some of the evaluation techniques—for example, how quickly, quietly, and efficiently the sniper could prepare for the first shot, which I called the elementary shot. This was always the most important shot of the session. Trainees could record the shots for themselves or through their NCO or supervisor, who might be a battalion squad leader, platoon leader, or team leader, as a baseline for subsequent training and performance. Their headquarters also wanted to maintain a progress record in their files, as we did at Fort Bragg, the 1st Special Forces, and often at the 14th Detachment.

The first exercise involved the foundational shot. This shot was at a hundred yards from a prone-supported position while the trainee engaged two identical "upper body" shots. The trainee could use a sling, tripod, sandbags, or any other available shooting aid.

The trainee sniper had unlimited time to place one center shot in the left portion of a target. He then reloaded and fired his second shot at the right portion of a target. Of course, we knew that there would be no practice or following shots in actual combat situations. Therefore, the initial shot tested both the shooter and his equipment and his ability to make the first shot count.

The second shot conditioned the shooter to reload and fire automatically. The target was then lowered and examined, to see if the shot was no more than two inches off the point of aim. That standard was realistic, because we used other weapons to zero the shots and the trainee was under no strain. He also had unlimited time and ideal conditions at that point.

The company carpenter, who was also an artist, and I constructed a typical enemy silhouette. We indicated how far the shooter needed to fire in front of a moving target at fifty yards and at a hundred yards. In other words, we indicated the lead. If the targets were running or walking, the lead distance was about twice as far.

We recorded the date, time, location, weapon, ammunition, wind velocity, and other relevant information. Then, we went to the next exercise from the prone-supported position. The student had unlimited time to fire five rounds at a small but clear aiming point on the target when shooting for the group. In other words, he shot for one particular point and saw how the five shots grouped around it. The purpose of this exercise was to test the consistency of the rifle, the scope, ammunition, and the shooter.

An axiom from Fort Bragg goes, "Accuracy is the product of uniformity." I told the group that if their target group was larger or more spread out than three inches, it should bother a good sniper with good equipment—and we had excellent equipment. For a new shooter with less than adequate equipment, we permitted a four-inch spread. However, three inches or less was the standard training goal. The common causes of poor grouping were loose screws and scope mounts and inferior ammunition. Of course, experience in shooting had a lot to do with it.

For command firing, the trainees had to load three rounds and, on command, fire one shot at an upper-body target. This was a shot from a supported prone position. They had to shoot within one second of the command and had to be in position and aiming at the target when the command came.

I used my .45-caliber pistol to indicate when to fire each round. I looked for consistent, centerhits on command. A good shooter would stay within a two-inch circle; however, anything in less than four inches would be effective.

For yard shooting (measured distance), we relocated to a two-hundred-yard line. The trainees then assumed a prone and supported position

quickly. By using known sight adjustments, held over from previous practice, I had them fire five head rounds. They had to do so as a timed and as a
command-fire exercise. The command was, "Five, four, three, two, one,
fire!" Some of the trainees had never officially fired beyond a hundred
yards, so this was quite a learning experience for them. The acceptable
standard for us was a center-hit shot in a four-to-six-inch group.

The next exercise shooting was three hundred yards from practice target.
The trainees had to fire five center shots on the same targets used for upper
body shot at two hundred yards. For an action shot, the trainees ran from a
two-hundred-yard line to a hundred-yard line and engaged the target with
five rounds of rapid fire in any supported (comfortable) position they
could find. We looked at the effects of stress and heavy breathing on the
shooters' scores. I stressed that push-ups, sit-ups, and rope climbing could
be used to improve breathing and heart rate.

The tactical exercises were a series of one and two shot drills performed
at varied unknown distances. They included shooting on roofs, from trees,
during field exercises, and while using certain types of camouflage. The
purpose of the exercises was to give the trainees information on bullet performance under varied and semi-scientific conditions.

In team training exercises, we made the point that the sniper is an integral part of the assault team training of the whole team. We emphasized
that rescue team training should be included in selected parts of sniper
team training.

We continually stressed the importance of taking care of the rifle.
Cleaning was the key. We told the trainees that the rifle was a precision
shooting machine and that incorrect cleaning would destroy the accuracy
of the rifle faster than an excessive amount of shooting. The barrel of the
rifle had to stay dry and ready for immediate deployment. Any solvent left
in the barrel would cause spontaneous shots to be off target.

As an added part of sniper training, we taught jungle walking. These
were exercises in patrolling, observing, and reacting while moving in
wooded areas. The drills took place in riverbeds and other accessible places
that lent themselves to this type of instruction.

We had trainees place targets in trees and ditches, fully or partially concealed, on each side of the trail. The future snipers moved down the predes-

ignated trails in a quiet but always alert manner. Each engaged targets as they became visible, taking cover, if available, and then continuing until we told them to halt the exercise. We also used a few simulated booby traps, trip wires, potholes, no-shoot targets, and homemade smoke pots. These devices proved effective in the ending phase of the training.

I encouraged trainees to exercise some "inventiveness" and organize some form of rifle competition for themselves. The specific type of rifle was unimportant. These competitions grew to be the sniper trainees' best form of stress training. They proved once again that there is no substitute for experience. At home base or wherever permitted, sniper trainees often had chances to compare equipment, training, and techniques. They drew upon each other's field experiences. They would also get practice opportunities, as we did back at Fort Bragg, to shoot under match conditions, under peer pressure, to get an accurate evaluation of skill levels.

Many senior commanders in various areas of the battalion often commented on the value of our training methods and the shooting programs. We considered our course an efficient use of training time.

Soon after our team left Laos, a "Declaration of Lao Neutrality" was signed and all foreign troops were supposed to leave. The White Star teams on the rotation following us returned to Fort Bragg and Okinawa, but the North Vietnamese increased their forces in Laos. A few years later, U.S. personnel returned to support the Hmong guerrillas under CIA civilian cover. The North Vietnamese use of the Laotian panhandle to supply their forces in South Vietnam made a mockery of the ostensible "neutrality." One of my closest friends, Staff Sgt. Chester D. Townsend, lost his life on 1 December 1963 during a TDY mission at Chau Lang, Vietnam. Chester was not a member of my immediate team, and I had returned to the United States before he died, but I was with him in spirit when I heard of his death, with my own Southeast Asian experience vividly in mind.

### Some "Lost Roles" of Special Forces

Lost in those dark jungles of the world, shrouded in the mists of the past, are mysteries about Special Forces operations that some are willing to accept. Many Americans try hard to forget everything that happened in Vietnam and the rest of Southeast Asia. Consequently, much of what occurred with the Special Forces there and throughout the world seems to have slipped into benign neglect.

At least our operations in Laos were highly successful. We proved that clandestine warfare had worked in the past and is highly effective. We knew at the time that, if the senior military and political leaders wanted to restrain or contain communism in the former Indochina, they needed to be a lot more imaginative and innovative than they seemed willing to be. They were wearing blinders. Certainly, none of our reports from the field corroborated their assessments.

# EPILOGUE

This is another type of war in its intensity, ancient in its origin—war by
guerrillas, subversives, insurgents, and assassins . . . seeking victory by
eroding and exhausting the enemy instead of engaging him.

John F. Kennedy, 1962

As my account of my experiences with Special Forces suggests, I perceived our operations as humanitarian in character, intended to evolve
into a positive force for the betterment of people's lives everywhere in the
world. I was not, I believe, alone in that perception. Collectively, we expected our unit to evolve into a combination of the soon-to-be Peace
Corps, a military and civil rehabilitation agent, an assessor of foreign political situations, and a corps of instructors in covert operations.

Because our hands-on experience in the field required every one of us to
master many skills and roles, when we thought of Special Forces as an institution we naturally envisioned those skills and roles as eventual institutional units. That is, each of us was a potential department in microcosm—
several departments, in fact. It is no wonder that we thought the wars of
the future would be fought on Special Forces terms.

At the same time, there appeared to be some disparity between the original Special Forces concept and what was demanded of us in the field. In direct combat with hostile forces, our notion of service acquired a sharper
edge. But even then we understood our main purpose to be the establishment of peace and order in embattled countries.

We should not dwell on events gone by, but we must not entirely forget
them. Exploring the history of Special Forces reveals some valuable lessons
learned in Southeast Asia. Formal histories are often deliberately distorted,
official secrets being only one reason for doing so. Any official record of

conflict may be riddled with ignorance, errors, misinterpretations, and the prejudices of journalists and historians. Personal histories, too, can be flawed. I offer here one soldier's firsthand experience, for whatever light it may shed on some dark but glorious years.

Readers will recall that in the 1950s all the nations of Southeast Asia were still recovering from the effects of wartime Japanese occupation and the ravages of World War II in the Pacific. Former colonies of Western nations struggled for stability as Russia and China pumped aid to communist insurgents determined to overcome weak nationalist governments.

The line between the day's events and the next day's needs could be balanced on the point of a .50-caliber bullet, as some observer is reputed to have said. Health and prosperity were not even memories for most of the population, who had known nothing but war of some kind for most of two decades (and would in fact see another decade of strife).

Special Forces came into being as a way of addressing that complex and unpredictable situation in line with the best interests of the United States, which included much more than merely promoting democratic principles over communist ones.

Our operational model and approach to the execution of missions in the 1950s helped the United States to resolve a dilemma of whether to support insurgencies or ignore them. We proved that operations of the type that Special Forces then pursued could provide the United States and the free world with a unique capacity to help bring peace and stability closer to many troubled areas. The sad part of the story is that our painfully learned lessons were not, in my view, sufficiently respected or applied in subsequent conflicts.

The American public needs to understand the original concept of Special Forces, and especially needs to know what we achieved. Special Forces accomplishments and contributions to national policy are not well understood. Imagine, junior officers and noncommissioned officers contributing significantly to national policy! It could be, however, that the public knows so little about Special Forces achievements because our mission was so difficult to grasp. In fact, it took a while for us to figure it out. And it kept changing.

### Envisioning the Future of Special Forces

Those of us who served with Special Forces in that precarious time could easily imagine just how important Special Forces operations of the future would be. The body of knowledge, the vocabulary, and the global outlook that we had developed amounted to a working primer for settling conflicts throughout the world.

I have had more than forty years to think about what Special Forces did and what we expected it to become. It has always seemed obvious to me that the United States badly needed to maintain an adequate staff of well-prepared and mission-experienced training cadre to teach the roles that Special Forces teams originally performed. The "multiplier" principle would always be valid, indeed necessary, to maintain U.S. influence overseas.

Special Forces appears to have evolved in other directions since I participated in the foundation and application of its original operational concepts. Thinking back to the unit's very beginning, I still believe strongly in its original philosophy. I also take note of ongoing concerns associated with growing organizational numbers. Special Forces now has become primarily a strike force.

Back then, though, we anticipated that there would eventually be a single Special Forces military control point (physical plant), the headquarters for global operations. (Our old home, Fort Bragg, North Carolina, would exist as headquarters for training and deployment.) Civilian and other oversight personnel would maintain ongoing liaison with the State Department as a worldwide operation.

This headquarters we envisioned would have its own organization and regulations for decision making, money spending, and troop deployment. It would forge military contacts with countries around the world, indirectly influencing foreign policy. There would be active training conducted abroad, from Africa to Cambodia to Mongolia to Fiji, and in hundreds of other countries. Emphasis would continue to be on diverse skills and flexibility for both trainers and trainees. Besides, there would be extensive instruction for nontraditional missions involving such areas as peacekeeping, drug interdiction, and humanitarian crises.

This visionary exercise anticipated some of the difficulties that might arise once foreign trainees returned to their own governments.

Understandings would need to be established with foreign powers regarding the use of Special Forces instruction within their borders. Inevitably, some countries would have uses for such training other than what the United States government anticipated. Some intelligence and counterintelligence operations would be required to monitor the situation.

Survival training and special training with foreign weapons and equipment was expected to continue. Teams could not effectively train personnel overseas with a lot of fancy American gear. If trainees used the old water-cooled 50-caliber machine guns, Springfield 02, and AK-47s (Mikhail T. Kalashnikov's assault rifle), Special Forces members would have to use the same during training and on missions. Training in the United States should familiarize trainees with the kind of environment that they might soon experience elsewhere, in terms of climate and living conditions. We knew that our trainers' basic requirements would need to include knowledge of the language and customs of countries involved.

In short, we imagined that Special Forces training would continue to provide the same kind of experiences that built the capabilities of the OSS in Europe and Burma in World War II. Routine training would continue in camouflage techniques, small-unit movement, troop-leading procedures, soldier-team development, rappelling, mountaineering, marksmanship, weapon maintenance, jungle warfare, first aid, day and night navigation, and paratrooper skills. Special Forces teams would also assist armies of nations around the world with senior administrative development.

Assuming that our functions would persist in our successors, we saw them first as teachers of indigenous Special Forces as trainer-multipliers; their second role would be teaching foreign internal defense (counter-insurgency). A third role resembled that of Rangers and other strike units, teaching countries how to defend themselves. One last role, but equally important, was serving as diplomatic emissaries, with full privileges and responsibilities in the field.

Meanwhile, of course, Special Forces would be fully trained in demolition, rescuing POWs and hostages, and penetrating deep behind enemy lines. We took for granted that if future Special Forces teams were expected to parachute in, attack a target, destroy it, and then leave, the establishment did not need us at all. It would need the 101st or 82d Airborne Division, or possibly the Rangers, but much more manpower than an A-Team.

We were especially interested in future official involvement in field mediation, because of our close contacts with local people in the field. We felt very strongly that headquarters-based decision-making attachés would not need to appear. A personal sense of the individuals involved would be more likely to achieve a good result. Such direct intervention, with the practical considerations facing the parties clearly before us, might have prevented our young women and men from dying thousands of miles from American soil.

Special Forces people would continue to mold field experiences into an American tradition. Such a tradition could be more powerful than any bomb yet devised. That tradition is the force of gentleness. We would continue to use it on a large scale. That was our picture of the future.

### Missed Opportunity

Because the evolution of Special Forces apparently did not agree with our recommendations from the field, the United States missed vital courses of action during the Vietnam War. Decision-makers failed to understand that they were facing a different type of war. They did not build on previous experience with jungle fighting, as a joint effort with local nationals. They did not welcome recommendations from field-tried jungle fighters. They failed to mobilize indigenous peoples effectively. They clung to conventional warfare organizational structures—tank battalions, infantry regiments, aviation brigades, etc.—without fully appreciating the multiplier concept: training local forces to train more.

Special Forces in the fifties documented conditions and trends that somehow failed to impress the decision-makers of the sixties; we will never know why they did not trust reports revealing why the people involved in those conflicts behaved the way they did. They did not use them to predict how the people would respond to U.S. intervention. A failure simply to study the Vietnamese people and their culture and history led to serious errors in judgment.

Above all, the situation in Southeast Asia in the fifties and sixties called for rapid adjustment to situational changes; the political process moved much too slowly to accommodate events in the field.

As a former Special Forces operative, I can only say that the high quality of the intelligence supplied by Special Forces during this period should have earned us more direct involvement in forming U.S. policy in the area.

### Lessons Learned

Given our visualization regarding the evolution of Special Forces, the following postulates apply:

employ Special Forces teams early into possible conflict situations;

consider recommendations of reports from the field about the people's values and morale as it exists in their "minds and hearts";

afford respect to all people and recognize their true human potential;

make sincere efforts to understand the political forces working within a country and within situations, including their inherent paradoxes and contradictions;

premise judgments on an understanding of nationalism—how "love of country" can impel people to fight to the death, person by person, family by family, village by village, and region by region;

realize that it takes more than words to explain *will to win;*

recognize the ideas and causes that compel people to action and generate the kind of devotion that existed in the "hearts and minds" of Japan during World War II—and in the American colonies at the time of our Revolution.

Effecting such recommendations depends on a willingness to study and fully understand the forces building in public forums in the field, rather than in the courtrooms and boardrooms. It also depends on continuing study of our history of covert and psychological warfare—in general, to study and take heed from the past. That is the only way to acquire total understanding of the difference between the government and the people of a country.

When Special Forces teams are deployed with an expressed intention of exposing countries to a democratic system, it is crucial to recognize that democracy itself is a culture. It proves itself in daily choices and custom.

Thus, as a country, we must always speak and act with truth and candor and listen—closely and sincerely—to all reports from the field.

### Looking Back

In the 1950s we had our thumbs on the pulse of the people. As we traveled through various villages and hamlets, most of the indigenous peoples of the areas reacted warmly toward us. We often forgot the looming communist insurgency facing that part of the world and only considered the possibilities our actions could create for the future. During that time most of the people knew our presence assured them of United States support and hope for the future.

We were right there on the ground during the early Vietnam affair and fully reported circumstances surrounding the "war." We furthermore were well aware of the situation in the field in the beginning of the conflict in Vietnam and reported that the struggle was with each woman, man, and child. The struggle in Vietnam was also throughout the country and not simply with the armed forces or government. We were aware, too, that the enemy would not give up and that the ideology they were fighting for was, although flawed, very powerful.

History lesson: President Lyndon B. Johnson appeared to consider advice from the field regarding the effectiveness of antiguerrilla operations during 1963. The rumor at the time was that the president deliberated strongly whether or not to expand covert efforts as a military strategy in Asia. There were those around him who tilted the scales and recommended otherwise, thus beginning the United States' military and industrial devastation approach in Asia.

We Special Forces veterans now talk about "the people." We talk about individuals, the whole of a society, and of our association with them. We witnessed the results of our caring and medical assistance; we saw it permeate their minds and hearts. We earned an intense camaraderie, mutual respect, and friendship. Strong bonds were forged. We saw proved again and again that the advantages of friendship cannot be fully developed from a distance.

Later on, the purpose and mission of the Special Forces appeared to shift. Only during the later and wider war did Special Forces appear to surface as mostly a fighting unit.

Even then, though, our team members worked tirelessly to help the people in these areas and to change the way the people perceived Americans and our lifestyle. Special Forces members motivated those brave survivors to live, to handle difficult situations, and in many cases to begin anew after a narrow escape from starvation or cholera or even war wounds.

Further study of our involvement and deployment of forces at the beginning of the Southeast Asia conflict is warranted, to help us understand and solve the political puzzles of the future, whenever any nation is threatened to be torn apart by conflict.

### Looking Ahead

Retaining the original ideology of Special Forces seems to me to be increasingly important because of the types of threats America continues to face.

The 14th Special Forces Operational Detachment predicted that teams could continue to help answer questions such as, "Can we do business with a particular country?" and "Are we putting areas such as trade before principles?" Our expectation was that the role of Special Forces would remain in the strategic spotlight after Vietnam. Instead of taking a backseat, the strategy we employed would continue as an important link of foreign policy.

This is important during any period of disorder. Now is a time of ethnic war and threats of mass destruction. We would be wise to rethink how this country should react to the kinds of conflicts it is likely to face in today's world.

We must be ready to fight a wide range of enemies in varied locations and terrain, and the United States should rethink conventional military doctrine. There must be continued scrutiny of the many approaches available for resolving conflicts. We should likewise analyze and debate fully all recommendations from the field.

As a last word, we should remember that Special Forces members served effectively as designated international field representatives and took on responsibilities that once belonged almost exclusively to military attachés. We need to profit directly from lessons learned in the field about spreading the influence of the United States. This includes discreetly forging new alliances and cultivating contracts among foreign leaders.

It is as clear today as it was then, that Special Forces should continue to play crucial roles in the future of America foreign policy. I strongly recommend that Special Forces team members continue to be serve the president, the State Department, and others as field attachés.

The Special Forces concept is much more complex than simply operational teams. It extends beyond day-to-day operations and allows influence at the highest levels of government and into the hearts and minds of a people. It is a philosophy of international collaboration.

All this is not to say that the United States should disband the armed forces or do away with traditional notions of applying overwhelming force. It does mean, however, that the nation should seriously consider all action alternatives.

The history of the 14th Special Forces Operational Detachment is a proud one. I am especially proud of my experiences. Today, I remember my Special Forces training, wear dog tags issued to me during basic training, and continue to treasure my first official beret, authorized in 1961. With me are mountains of memories that will never fade away.

## About the Author

Chalmers Archer Jr. is the author of *Growing Up Black in Rural Mississippi*, the 1993 winner of the Mississippi Institute of Arts and Letters Award for nonfiction. A former professor and college community relations director at Northern Virginia Community College in Alexandria, Virginia, he has taught at all levels, from elementary to postgraduate studies, and served as a guest lecturer at Cambridge University. He earned his B.S. and M.Ed. at the Tuskegee Institute in 1972 and a doctorate from Auburn University in 1979, completing postgraduate work at the University of Alabama the following year.

Dr. Archer is a member of the Democratic Speakers Bureau and has worked with several national politicians, including Bill Clinton, Bob Dole, and Ron Brown. In his spare time, Dr. Archer is a motivational speaker for minority and youth groups.

**The Naval Institute Press** is the book-publishing arm of the U.S. Naval Institute, a private, nonprofit, membership society for sea service professionals and others who share an interest in naval and maritime affairs. Established in 1873 at the U.S. Naval Academy in Annapolis, Maryland, where its offices remain today, the Naval Institute has members worldwide.

Members of the Naval Institute support the education programs of the society and receive the influential monthly magazine *Proceedings* and discounts on fine nautical prints and on ship and aircraft photos. They also have access to the transcripts of the Institute's Oral History Program and get discounted admission to any of the Institute-sponsored seminars offered around the country.

The Naval Institute also publishes *Naval History* magazine. This colorful bimonthly is filled with entertaining and thought-provoking articles, first-person reminiscences, and dramatic art and photography. Members receive a discount on *Naval History* subscriptions.

The Naval Institute's book-publishing program, begun in 1898 with basic guides to naval practices, has broadened its scope to include books of more general interest. Now the Naval Institute Press publishes about one hundred titles each year, ranging from how-to books on boating and navigation to battle histories, biographies, ship and aircraft guides, and novels. Institute members receive significant discounts on the Press's more than eight hundred books in print.

Full-time students are eligible for special half-price membership rates. Life memberships are also available.

For a free catalog describing Naval Institute Press books currently available, and for further information about subscribing to *Naval History* magazine or about joining the U.S. Naval Institute, please write to:

Membership Department
**U.S. Naval Institute**
291 Wood Road
Annapolis, MD 21402-5034
Telephone: (800) 233-8764
Fax: (410) 269-7940
Web address: www.usni.org